Psychotherapy in an Age of Narcissism

Also by Joel Paris

BORDERLINE PERSONALITY DISORDER: Etiology and Treatment (*editor*)

BORDERLINE PERSONALITY DISORDER: A Multidimensional Approach

SOCIAL FACTORS IN THE PERSONALITY DISORDERS: A Biopsychosocial Approach to Etiology and Treatment

WORKING WITH TRAITS: Psychotherapy of Personality Disorders

NATURE AND NURTURE IN PSYCHIATRY: A Predisposition-Stress Model

MYTHS OF CHILDHOOD

PERSONALITY DISORDERS OVER TIME: Precursors, Course, and Outcome

THE FALL OF AN ICON: Psychoanalysis and Academic Psychiatry

HALF IN LOVE WITH DEATH: Managing the Chronically Suicidal Patient

PRESCRIPTIONS FOR THE MIND: A Critical View of Contemporary Psychiatry

TREATMENT OF BORDERLINE PERSONALITY DISORDER: A Guide to Evidence-Based Practice

THE USE AND MISUSE OF PSYCHIATRIC DRUGS: An Evidence-Based Critique

THE BIPOLAR SPECTRUM: Diagnosis or Fad?

Psychotherapy in an Age of Narcissism

Modernity, Science, and Society

Joel Paris
McGill University, Canada

palgrave
macmillan

First published 2013 by
PALGRAVE MACMILLAN

Palgrave Macmillan in the UK is an imprint of Macmillan Publishers Limited, registered in England, company number 785998, of Houndmills, Basingstoke, Hampshire RG21 6XS.

Palgrave Macmillan in the US is a division of St Martin's Press LLC, 175 Fifth Avenue, New York, NY 10010.

Palgrave Macmillan is the global academic imprint of the above companies and has companies and representatives throughout the world.

ISBN 978–0–230–33696–4

This book is printed on paper suitable for recycling and made from fully managed and sustained forest sources. Logging, pulping and manufacturing processes are expected to conform to the environmental regulations of the country of origin.

A catalogue record for this book is available from the British Library.

A catalog record for this book is available from the Library of Congress.

10 9 8 7 6 5 4 3 2 1
22 21 20 19 18 17 16 15 14 13

Printed and bound in the United States of America

This book is dedicated to my grandchildren, Madeleine, Noah, Simon, and Miriam

Contents

Preface

What This Book Is about

Millions of people have been in psychotherapy. Patients with a wide range of psychological problems come to talk about their lives. But psychotherapy is more than a clinical tool. It has become an icon of contemporary society. The *ideas* behind therapy permeate our culture.

The main thesis of this book is that the "talking cure" is a product of the *modern* world, in which collective attachments are weaker and in which individual needs have become paramount. This book will also underline the problem of *cultural narcissism*: a social trend leading people to focus more on their inner psyche and personal needs, and less on commitments to family, community, and society. Modern people may pursue "self-esteem" in a vacuum, instead of rooting a sense of self in commitments and connections to the outside world. The assumption that raising self-esteem is good for mental health can be so pervasive that neither therapists nor patients notice it.

Sigmund Freud, when asked how he conceptualized mental health, answered simply, "love and work". By and large, that is what talking therapy promotes. When the treatment *itself* turns into an exercise promoting personal and cultural narcissism, it works against its own goals. Reviewing the past, present, and future of talking therapy, I will show why psychotherapists and their patients need to be aware of these problems. The goal of talking about oneself should be to move beyond preoccupation with personal needs, and to belong to something outside the self. In common parlance, this is called "getting a life".

Like most mental health professionals, I am an individualist who cherishes personal freedom. The world of the past provided tradition and structure, but was overly restrictive and oppressive. Yet even though I am a lifelong liberal, conservative values are required for what is worth conserving. We need to find a balance between alienation and integration.

This book will also draw on a large body of empirical data showing when and how talking therapies heal. Too much writing on psychotherapy contains little but clinical opinion. Science has the capacity to measure and to explain subjective psychological states. The problem is that research has not consistently risen to this challenge, and modern clinical science tends to reduce all mental activity to neurons and chemical neurotransmitters. The book will also make clear that psychotherapy is an art that cannot be reduced to procedures, manuals, or techniques. Finally, it will make use of the social science literature, again favoring empirical work that describes the context in which psychotherapy is practiced.

This book has been written for practicing therapists but should be of interest to the educated public. Since many of these potential readers will have been in psychotherapy, they can draw on their own experiences as consumers of mental health services.

How I Came to Write This Book

I have been a psychiatrist for over 40 years. When I was a young medical graduate in training to be a specialist, psychotherapy was the central tool of the profession. That is no longer the case. The majority of psychiatrists define themselves as experts in prescribing medication, while psychologists and other mental health professionals provide most psychotherapy services.

Like other psychiatrists, I have moved with the times. I do more consultations, provide less direct treatment, and prescribe more drugs. The hegemony of psychoanalysis is a distant memory. But I still actively use psychotherapy. The reason is that the patients that I am most interested in (those diagnosed with personality disorders) do not benefit greatly from medication, but respond to specific forms of psychological treatment.

While my clinical experiences have led me to value psychotherapy, I have had to come to terms with its limitations and problems. I have seen too many patients go endlessly to therapists, searching for answers that treatment cannot provide. I sometimes see psychotherapy make people worse, not better. The reasons reflect much about the society we live in, and what people expect from their lives.

In psychotherapy, patients try to heal themselves by talking, but can end up trapped in a labyrinth of self. Their dialogue with the wider world takes place in front of a mirror. Patients come to talk about themselves, but therapists need to engage them in dialogue, and ensure that they are not just talking *to* themselves.

Acknowledgments

Since this book straddles psychiatry, psychology, and social science, I needed feedback from critical readers in other disciplines. Frank Furedi, who was a peer reviewer, was particularly helpful with sociological issues. Roz Paris and Hallie Frank read earlier drafts, and David Goldbloom, who reviewed the book in its later stages, helped to shape its final form.

Part I

The World of Psychotherapy

1
The Birth of Psychotherapy

Millions have sought psychotherapy. Talking as a way of healing that is psychotherapy, has become an important part of contemporary culture. Yet the ideas behind this kind of treatment are modern. Psychotherapy as a formal discipline and procedure was only invented a little more than a hundred years ago. We need to understand why talking therapy appeared at a particular moment of history and what function it serves in modern society.

In the course of history, every society has developed its own way of providing solace for psychological distress. In the past, people found help in other ways. They obtained comfort from religious institutions, community, and social networks. In traditional Western societies, troubled individuals could confess to a priest. In non-Western societies they might go through healing rituals with a shaman. But while all societies carry out some form of mental healing, these procedures cannot be termed as psychotherapy, and their effectiveness has never been tested empirically.

What is new today is that people are prepared to talk about personal problems to a professional. No one in a traditional society would have dreamed of doing so. But in the modern world, as older ways of healing stopped working, a new method had to be invented.

Modernity, individualism, and narcissism

The appearance of psychotherapy corresponded with the emergence of a different type of society. The term *modernity* describes cultural changes associated with a decline in traditional norms (Giddens, 1998). The modern world prizes the individual, and encourages people to look inward rather than outward for guidance. In this way, talking therapy is a product of modern culture. One of the principal characteristics of modernity is *individualism*, a preference for what benefits the self over the collective (Rieff, 1966). This social value has greatly shaped the psychotherapeutic enterprise.

At the same time, psychotherapy too has contributed to modernity. Several observers have commented on this relationship. Gross (1978) described the development of a "psychological society", and Rieff (1966) spoke of a "triumph of the therapeutic". One common thread in the observations is that values have come to depend on inner states rather than on external reality. Furedi (2004) observed that in the modern world, our very sense of identity and self has come to depend on the state of our psyche. One question that this book will address is whether the cultural role of psychotherapy has overshadowed its use as a healing procedure.

The modern celebration of the individual is a prerequisite for conducting formal psychotherapy, in which patients focus more on inner states of mind than on filling social roles. But focusing too much on the self has a "dark side". *Narcissism* is a psychological construct that describes the self-love and self-absorption that arise from an excess of individualism.

Sigmund Freud (1914–1959) was the first person to use this term, which is derived from a Greek legend, in a consistent theoretical paradigm. Freud conceived of narcissism as more of a universal psychological mechanism than as a problem. But later writers used narcissism to describe a pathological personality structure (Kohut, 1970). Since narcissism is a personality trait that varies from one person to another, it is possible to study it empirically (Thomaes et al., 2009). Finally, Lasch (1979) introduced the concept of *cultural narcissism* to describe how excessive focus on the self can undermine personal and social cohesion.

The concept of narcissism is not really new. Vanity has always been considered by religions to be sinful. Few approve of people who are excessively conceited or self-centered. But the modern world has given narcissism a new twist. As an extreme version of individualism, it has come to be celebrated by a culture that rewards and values ambition, celebrity, and "self-esteem".

Psychotherapy, by its very nature, runs the risk of promoting narcissism. This is an inevitable result of spending many hours talking about oneself to a sympathetic, non-judgmental listener. By losing sight of social roles and social networks, psychotherapy in the 20th century became a subversive force. In summary, the role of psychotherapy in modern society is historically contingent. Thus, its rise can only be understood in the context of the social changes that accompanied modernity.

Filling a niche

Psychotherapy did not emerge all at once. Its 19th-century precursors were various methods for the cure of "nervous" ailments (Ellenberger, 1970; Shorter, 1997; Caplan, 1998; Engel, 2008). Such treatments, usually prescribed by physicians, included rest cures at spas to recover from nervous exhaustion, which was called "neurasthenia" (Schuster, 2003). Obviously such an option was open only to the wealthy. And many of these healing procedures lay outside of medicine and were based on religious principles, often assuming a prior commitment to Christianity (Moskowitz, 2001).

In fact psychological treatment in the 19th century lacked most of the features that have, ever since Freud, characterized the "talking cure". Patients were not invited to sit down and talk without explicit direction. They were not "heard" in the way that psychotherapists now take for granted. Instead, they were directed to activities designed to distract them from their problems. These procedures did not always work. There was room for a radically different approach.

The Austrian neurologist Sigmund Freud is generally acknowledged to be the founder of psychotherapy. He deserves great credit for this. Even if his specific theories and methods are now obsolete, it was Freud who made talking therapy influential, it was he whose ideas caught on with a wide public, and it was he who had the greatest influence on modern culture. All psychotherapies that explore the mind through active listening are derived from him.

But why did psychoanalysis emerge at the turn of the 20th century? What was special about that time? One possibility is that this was the historical moment when modernization reached a tipping point. Over several centuries, modern society gradually replaced traditional social structures, and individual values became predominant over collective values. Thus psychotherapy (and the ideas behind it) had its greatest success in societies in which individualism and modernity were most prominent, particularly in the United States (Caplan, 1998).

Talking therapy succeeded because it filled an empty niche. Community, tradition, and faith were in decline. Many felt lost in a world they had not made. People had to establish their own roles and their own social networks. Most found a niche, but many remained alienated. Moreover, in capitalist society, strong individualistic values became associated with a level of social inequality that made many unhappy (Wilkinson and Pickett, 2009).

But the most serious problem was that as external guidelines for behavior weakened, people had to look inward. Older methods of healing had lost their power. Talking therapy promoted the idea that exploring, understanding, and controlling the mind was the best way of meeting personal goals. In this way, psychotherapy became a necessary part of modern culture. It has even been conceptualized as an answer to the human condition—a kind of "civil religion" (Epstein, 2006).

Mental symptoms and traditional healing

Mental symptoms have been described since the first written historical records were created. In the Bible (Psalm 38) one finds this description of melancholic depression: "I am troubled, I am bowed down greatly; I go mourning all the day long.... I groan because of the turmoil of my heart." In the 4th century BC, Hippocrates described a depressed patient in this way: "A woman of Thasos became morose, and although she did not take to her bed, she suffered from insomnia, loss of appetite...she complained of fears and talked much; she showed despondency and talked at random" (Adams, 1939).

Psychological symptoms are universal, and serve a purpose in communicating distress (Nesse and Williams, 1995). But when symptoms interfere with functioning, those who suffer from them require help. In Shakespeare's play with the same title, Macbeth, troubled by his wife's depression, asks a question that might be put to any modern psychotherapist: "Cans't thou not minister to a mind diseas'd; Pluck from memory a rooted sorrow...?" The physician replies: "Therein the patient must minister to himself."

In spite of Shakespeare's doubts, healing rituals have been documented in virtually every culture. But to understand traditional healing, we need to imagine a very different world from the one we live in. People in traditional societies did not see themselves as much as individuals as they saw themselves as part of a social community (Kirmayer, 2007). Most people in the course of human history have lived in villages, where they have probably known less than a hundred people over a lifetime. They have been more deeply engaged with their community than with people in modern urban society.

Comfort for the afflicted has always been one of the primary functions of religion. In shamanism, "evil spirits" are banished through an extended ritual. But the real function of such procedures is to mobilize family members and the larger community to support the sufferer (Kirmayer, 2004). Prior to modernity, suffering was understood in a religious context, and healing rites were carried out in the context of a shared belief system. Relief from psychic pain could occur if symptoms were given meaning, and if social support could be increased. This process still goes on at places such as the shrine of Lourdes (Frank and Frank, 1991).

In contrast, modern methods of healing are totally secular. There are still rituals, as in the schedule and routine of a psychotherapy session. But healing is now rooted in a different worldview. Traditional attachments to community and shared belief systems tend to be attenuated rather than supported, leading to an increased focus on personal needs (Westen, 1988). Psychotherapy makes people more, not less, individualistic.

People also experience distress in different ways than they used to do in the past. Research shows that those who are less integrated with their community tend to have fewer *internalizing* problems, that is distress within the self, but more *externalizing* problems, that is behaviors with other people (Paris, 2004). But inner suffering is what talking therapy was designed to deal with.

For most of human history, little has been done for people who have suffered from severe mental disorders—other than confinement. Today while medical treatment is highly useful for severely ill patients, these methods have only become available in recent decades. Treatment for psychosis in the past was neither benign nor helpful—the mentally ill were often mistreated and abused (Shorter, 1997; Wallace, 2008). And if recovery did not occur quickly, the community could reject them.

The view of Michel Foucault (2001) that serious mental illnesses were tolerated and widely accepted in the past and that traditional societies viewed psychosis as little more than eccentricity was an unhistorical fantasy. Such ideas are based on a sentimental view of the past—a modern version of the old conundrum that life used to be simpler and happier.

Most people in distress experience mild symptoms that affect their states of mind without seriously impairing their social functioning (Kessler et al., 2005a). People with these problems may not seek professional treatment (Kessler et al., 2005b). And they are not wrong to decline to become patients. One way or another, most of us pull out of a temporary tailspin. Time does heal—as does the support of family, friends, and community. That is how people have dealt with distress throughout history.

How psychotherapy was born

Formal psychotherapy began with psychoanalysis. Its theories may initially have been startling, but they had many historical precedents (Ellenberger, 1970; Hale, 1995). What was really new was the psychoanalytic method, based on the idea that talking can heal psychological conflict and distress. Freud was the first therapist to advocate listening to people in an open and unprejudiced way. He was also the first to understand that psychotherapy encounters are emotionally charged and personally meaningful. Finally, he was the first to read between the lines of personal discourse and to take into account the discrepancy between what people say and what they really think.

Freud's ideas were developed at a time when organized religion was already in decline. Confession in the Catholic Church has a certain similarity to psychoanalysis in that people obtain solace by confiding in a trusted person. It may not have been an accident that Freud, who lived in a Catholic society, kept out of sight behind a couch, much like a priest. But confession is a very different procedure from psychotherapy.

The common thread is that people feel better after confiding in someone who listens and understands. Not everyone can find that kind of support outside of psychotherapy. When you explain your feelings to a friend or a family member, they may stop you to give their opinion or tell their own stories. The idea of sharing your troubles with a professional about whom you know nothing but in whom you confide everything, and who empathizes with your feelings and also sometimes offers solutions to problems, was novel indeed.

Methods of psychotherapy

Psychoanalysis is the form of psychotherapy that has had the greatest cultural impact. Freudian theories paralleled developments in culture and the arts, sharing a focus on hidden but powerful emotions. These ideas were, and still are, attractive to intellectuals (Wilson, 2003). The success of psychoanalysis was, at least in part, due to good timing. Its ideas had few serious competitors and were seen as reflecting the most advanced concepts in psychology (Hale, 1995). Moreover, treatment in the early days of psychoanalysis was not prohibitively expensive. Even struggling artists were able to afford the fees. Along with appreciation of the latest trends in art and literature, being "in analysis" may have made people feel "modern" (Hale, 1995).

But there was a deeper reason for the popularity of psychoanalysis. The British philosopher Ernest Gellner (1993) suggested that this form of treatment was designed to address a problem particular to the contemporary world: insecurity in relation to social status and attachments. This helps to explain why it appeared at the same historical moment as rapid social change and modernity.

The movement that Freud founded (as well as its descendants and variants) had its greatest success in the United States, but aroused greater resistance wherever tradition remained strong. Freudian ideas took a long time to catch on in Europe, where the culture was more stable and where people retained a greater sense of belonging. Only recently, as Europeans became as modern as Americans, did psychoanalysis become popular there (Zaretsky, 2004).

Psychoanalysis, unlike traditional healing, did not aim to reintegrate people into a collectivity, as religion had done. Instead, it encouraged them to become more successfully individualistic. Its thrust was to make people become less dependent on their social environment. Yet as Cushman (1995) was the first to observe, that is precisely the reason why talking therapy always runs the risk of *worsening* the very problems it sets out to solve. The more people focus on the self and inner feelings, the less sensitive they tend to be to others. In this way, talking therapy runs the constant danger of supporting narcissism, at both the individual and the cultural levels.

And that is only one of the several downsides of the social impact of psychotherapy. As Furedi (2004) has observed, the culture of therapy has come to redefine what it means to be a person. This culture tends to view the self as emotionally vulnerable and powerless in the face of circumstance. But seeing every dilemma through the lens of therapy turns social issues into psychological problems. It is a point of view that threatens to turn history into therapy, trivializing real social problems.

How psychotherapy became a profession

To be seen as legitimate, psychotherapy had to become a profession. Professionalization was necessary to separate formal treatment from lay advice. Even now, the boundary is not always clear. Since the middle of the 19th century, advice columns have enjoyed enormous popularity in the media (Cushman, 1995). It is hard to imagine people in traditional societies seeking help for life problems from complete strangers. Yet today, hardly any newspaper lacks an advice column. While therapists have sometimes taken these columns over, the most popular ones in the United States, such as "Dear Abby", "Ann Landers", and their successors, offer advice by savvy journalists.

Professionalization was a long and complex process. In 19th-century medicine, there was no such thing as a specialty of psychiatry (Shorter, 1997). Physicians treating inpatients admitted to mental hospitals were called "alienists" or "neuropsychiatrists". For outpatients, there were neurologists who focused on "neurotic" patients. Freud was one of them, as was George Miller Beard, an American physician who developed a rest cure for what was called "neurasthenia". Psychiatry as a separate specialty emerged later, only gradually separating itself from neurology (Berrios and Porter, 1995).

Clinical psychology was also slow to define itself as a profession (Benjamin, 2007). At the turn of the 20th century, the discipline was founded by Lightner Witmer (who initiated the child guidance movement) and by G. Stanley Hall (who developed educational psychology and the modern concept of adolescence). But for many years, clinical psychologists were more interested in assessment than treatment. Academic departments of psychology, which focus on research, have rarely been very interested in training clinicians. Even today, there is controversy as to whether psychologists who do therapy really need a PhD or whether they should have experience in research (Dawes, 1994).

The involvement of social workers in psychotherapy is a more recent development (Strean, 1974), but these professionals have come to form the largest single group of practitioners (Weissman et al., 2006). To claim a separate identity, social workers originally described their approach as "case work". Some went on to train as psychoanalysts, but others focused on family therapy (a field they continue to dominate). Most social workers pride themselves on their focus on practical, here-and-now issues, rather than on grand theories.

Therapists can come from backgrounds that are far removed from medicine or psychology, sometimes having no previous background at all in the mental health professions. In recent years, professors of literature have been allowed to enter psychoanalytic training, mainly to keep training institutes open in an era when few psychiatrists or clinical psychologists choose to become analysts. In rare but prominent cases (for example Erik Erikson), a therapist might have no university degree at all.

Psychotherapy itself has never been a profession. Most of its practitioners have a degree in another discipline. That is why they need supervised clinical experience to begin to practice. Obviously, much has to be learned "on the job". And since there is no unified structure for therapy as a whole, anybody can start up a new therapy if they decide to. (As the next chapter will show, that is exactly what has happened.) Moreover, anyone with a PhD in any subject can still call himself "Doctor", creating confusion about what that qualification means.

The classical example was Freud himself. Rejected by academic medicine, and with no formal training in the treatment of mental disorders, he formed freestanding psychoanalytic institutes. Freud welcomed therapists from many backgrounds and viewed analysis as a separate discipline outside of medicine. Today, therapists who want to go their own way can do the same thing by creating an "Institute" for training that offers credentials by a defined method.

In the absence of a unifying structure, formal links are lacking between psychotherapy and the academic world. Thus, while almost all psychotherapists are professionals, no cohesive structure has developed for the field as a whole. This is why psychotherapy will eventually need to define itself as a separate profession. As it stands, endless fragmentation bedevils the field. Theoretical and practical disputes have led to repeated splintering of psychotherapy, both as a theory and as a discipline. And when science is lacking, entrepreneurship fills the gap.

Science, marketing, and the consumer

Most psychotherapists work in an environment that is not conducive to research. If they conduct solo practice, they can talk to colleagues, read a little, and go to a few conferences every year. But there is a large gap between science and practice. Instead of testing theories scientifically, most methods are rooted in armchair speculation and entirely lack a grounding in empirical data or clinical trials. (The main exception, as we will see, is cognitive behavioral therapy, or CBT.)

Critics have used the absence of evidence regarding efficacy to discredit psychotherapy. Much of this criticism has been directed at psychoanalysis, which has very little supporting data (Torrey, 1992). The same critique can be applied to many other methods of talking therapy. All therapies need to be scientifically validated if they wish to be taken seriously.

Moreover, as long as psychotherapy remains fragmented into "schools of thought", consumers face a confusing range of choices. Unfortunately, prospective patients have no recourse to an independent body of experts for guidance. (There is no equivalent of *Consumer Reports* for psychotherapy seekers.) The constant creation of new therapies, few of which are subjected to testing, continues apace. The creators of each method write books and give workshops to practitioners that describe their ideas. Marketing, not science, has become the measure of success. In this way, psychotherapy can be considered to be more of a business than a profession.

The underlying problem is that psychotherapies do not have a gold standard; therefore its practitioners lack the level of consensus that is found in medicine. You can see ten therapists and be offered ten different treatments. Yet many of the differences between therapy methods are illusory. What research shows is that the commonalities among all psychotherapies were and are enormous (Wampold, 2007). It makes little difference whether you lie on a couch or sit in an armchair. Even more importantly, the ideas that therapists believe in do not seem to make much of a difference to the results. It may not matter what the theory is, if the therapist has a talent for helping others. And even if every form of treatment has a toolkit of one kind or another, efficacy depends less on technique and more on the capacity to create a trusting and empathic relationship. Even so, as the next chapter will show, some therapies, particularly the most faddish ones, can cause real harm. Consumers need to know that talking is not always benign.

Psychotherapy and science

Talking therapy exists in a culture more and more influenced by science. Like any other clinical method, it must prove that it works. No one should pay for treatment without that assurance. Psychoanalysis had little interest in research, which is one of the main reasons why it went into decline. Without clinical trials to show effectiveness, no one can be expected to make a large investment of time and money (Paris, 2005).

In contrast, CBT earned much of its current prestige by conducting, from the very beginning, systematic investigations of its efficacy. A former analyst, Aaron Beck (1986), developed this method, which is now the most prominent form of talking therapy. It is the only form of psychotherapy that is supported by a large body of research.

When practitioners saw that clinical trials supported CBT, many changed their allegiance. The race was between a tortoise (CBT, cautiously moving forward) and a hare (psychoanalysis, leaping ahead overconfidently). Research gradually built a powerful case for CBT. One day, psychoanalysis woke up and found it had lost out. Even so, the effectiveness of CBT need not depend on its theoretical structure. It may just be particularly good at mobilizing the common factors that make all therapies work.

The culture of research is very different from that of the clinical world. A researcher is trained to *doubt* everything. In contrast, clinicians are expected to exude optimism and certainty. Very few have been able to bridge this gap. One could fill several floors of a large library with all the books that have been written about psychotherapy. But if one were to limit one's collection to books and articles based on research findings, a small room would be sufficient.

Empirical research supports the prescription of psychotherapy for specific patients with specific problems. Yet talking therapy is no panacea. Sometimes it does work and sometimes it does not. And bad therapy has the power to make patients worse. Moreover, talking therapy might have been a passing fad if it had remained rooted entirely in clinical experience and the advocacy of its practitioners. Its failure to present itself as a unified discipline and its fragmentation into multiple schools of thought, each of which reflects the narcissism and financial interests of its creator, brought it deserved discredit. Moreover, therapy brought much justified criticism on itself by claiming to be an answer to the human condition. In the end, psychotherapy must stand or fall on whether it can be proven to heal suffering.

2
Schools of Psychotherapy

Few things are standard in the modern world. Practitioners do not agree on any single method of psychotherapy. Instead, patients are forced to choose from a wide range of "boutique" options. Confusingly, each claims to be unique and is marketed as such—often using a three-letter acronym to impress prospective customers. Modern culture tends to encourage consumers to try "the latest thing". Sometimes the field seems a "free for all", in which anything goes.

Ever since it appeared on the scene, psychotherapy has been divided and fragmented into multiple "schools" (Borch-Jacobsen, 2009). Each competing method originated with a founding leader, in a kind of "guru" model. Each founder attracted disciples, promoted ideas to other clinicians through workshops, and then wrote books for consumers.

While each method is marketed as unique, most schools of therapy conduct no research and report no empirical data on efficacy. Instead of participating in the rigorous hypothesis testing that characterizes science, therapeutic gurus simply *illustrate* their theories with case examples. By and large, therapists, who are rarely trained in science, prefer to tell *stories*—preferably tales of miraculous cures.

Schools of thought are *pre-scientific*—a term famously introduced by the American philosopher Thomas Kuhn (1970). Kuhn observed that science works within a *paradigm*, that is, a working model that produces hypotheses that can be tested empirically. In the end, the model stands or falls on what evidence shows. The scientific method does *not* make use of case histories, which can only count as anecdotes. Or, as a common witticism puts it: *the plural of anecdote is not data.*

For most of its history, psychotherapy has been a clinical art, and the use of scientific methods to assess efficacy is a relatively recent development (Lambert, 2003). But since talking therapy can be an expensive, time-consuming, and risky procedure, it should be tested with the same methods that are applied to drugs. That usually means randomized clinical trials that compare results of treatment to no treatment or to a competing treatment.

Schools are so well entrenched as a feature of psychotherapy that patients may ask therapists which one they belong to. Some years ago, I was treating a college teacher who met standard criteria for a diagnosis of narcissistic personality disorder. He taught a film course that applied the theories of the radical French psychoanalyst Jacques Lacan. My patient could not understand why I did not have my own guru—as he did. I was unable to convince him that *not* belonging to a school was a good thing.

Schools of thought have had much more influence on practice than research. Thus, as the joke goes, instead of evidence-based therapy, we have had *eminence-based* therapy. This level of fragmentation would not be tolerated in psychopharmacology. There could never be anything like a Prozac school or a Valium school of drug treatment. Nor should there be.

How schools developed

Most of the problems that afflict the current therapy scene began with Freud. His treatment was rooted in a few theoretical principles: an unconscious mind, conflict between mental functions, the influence of childhood experiences on adult life, the tendency of therapy to elicit some of the same problems seen in other relationships, and a cure that depended on understanding all these mechanisms. Unfortunately Freud became a charismatic leader of a cult who did not tolerate dissent (Webster, 1995). And he never seriously considered that the analytic method needed to be subjected to quantitative evaluation. He did not believe that data consisting of numbers could ever be comparable to the insights gained by simply listening to patients.

To be fair, Freud did not differ from most of his contemporaries. Medicine in his time was only partly based on systematic research, and practice depended almost exclusively on experience. William Osler, the greatest physician of that time, used a "data base" almost entirely based on clinical observation (Osler, 1898). Controlled trials of medical treatment would not be conducted for another 50 years.

The problem with detailed study of a few cases is that conclusions cannot be generalized. This is why, from the beginning, the power and influence of each method of psychotherapy has depended on the charisma and influence of its founder. There was no basis for "believing in" psychoanalysis, or any other method, other than accepting authority (and trying out ideas in one's own practice). Moreover, anyone who follows a specific method tends to find what he or she is looking for (Baron, 2000). Psychotherapy provides many opportunities to confirm preconceived ideas—and to reduce "cognitive dissonance" (Festinger, 1957; Aronson, 1969).

Psychoanalysis had some clever built-in mechanisms for dismissing criticism. Patients who did not agree with the treatment must be demonstrating "resistance". Like a religious dogma, it was a closed system that could not be refuted. Theory and practice could only be changed after the founder's death. Even then, advocates performed Talmudic sleights of hand, claiming that any new ideas were expansions, not refutations, of Freud.

The science and practice of psychotherapy have not been closely linked to the academic world, the very place where it was most likely to receive constructive criticism. In the case of psychoanalysis, even sympathetic academics learned that deviations were not to be tolerated. Eugen Bleuler, the early 20th-century Swiss professor of psychiatry who introduced the word "schizophrenia", had to resign from a psychoanalytic society when he refused to support Freud's sexual theories (Decker, 2008).

In a university, academic debate is intense, and although sometimes painful, controversy is good for science. When a school of thought develops its own independent structure, orthodoxy usually rules. Freud began a pattern, followed by most of the schools that emerged for training therapists in *institutes* and maintaining their allegiance through *societies* (Hale, 1995). In the long run, this policy led to intellectual isolation, destroyed creativity, and contributed to the decline of psychoanalysis. In the end, without scientific support for a method, potential consumers will lose faith and look elsewhere.

Schools lead inevitably to fragmentation. The various psychotherapies that emerged often look more like religious sects than competing scientific ideas. In contrast, when interfaces with other disciplines are explored, the outcome can be creative. For example, the British psychiatrist John Bowlby (1969, 1973, 1980) developed *attachment theory* by collaborating with academic psychologists who developed ways to measure his constructs empirically. Today, this is the predominant strain in psychoanalysis, and attachment theory has produced a large research literature that has profoundly influenced developmental psychology (Cassidy and Shaver, 2009) as well as clinical practice (Fonagy, 2001).

However, in spite of theoretical advances, there is no evidence that psychotherapy based on attachment theory is any more effective.

Psychotherapy fads

When clinical opinion takes precedence over empirical data, therapy can be plagued by fads. And these are the kind of treatments that can do harm to patients. There have been many such fads over the last century. Some receded from the scene once their founders grew old or died, for example transactional analysis (Berne, 1964), gestalt therapy (Perls, 1969), or primal scream therapy (Janov, 1970). But new ones keep popping up.

Let us begin by considering two illustrative examples, one not that far from the mainstream and another whose rationale and procedures fly in the face of scientific knowledge. The first, eye movement desensitization and reprocessing (EMDR; Shapiro, 1995), can be called a faddish therapy because it is no better than existing methods but has been more skillfully marketed. The second, "recovered memory therapy", is a mélange of bizarre techniques that has done serious harm to patients.

The fad for EMDR occurred at a time when therapists became interested in the diagnosis of post-traumatic stress disorder (PTSD). This diagnosis is itself something of a fad, since traumatic events do not consistently produce symptoms (McNally, 2003). A psychologist, Francine Shapiro (1995), developed a technique that seemed to bring Freud up to date. Patients were asked to re-experience traumatic events to allow them to be "processed". Actually, re-imagining of experiences has long been used in cognitive therapy. The twist of EMDR was to enhance reprocessing by asking the patient to carry out eye movements under the guidance of the therapist. In a videotape of an EMDR session that I viewed, the therapist waved a wand in front of the patient while she remembered traumatic experiences. I was immediately reminded of Anton Mesmer's hypnotic approach to patients in the 18th century (Ellenberger, 1970). Evidently, what Mesmer called "animal magnetism" is alive and well in our own time.

Any new technique, if marketed properly, can become "hot". EMDR, to its credit, stimulated a fair body of research (over 500 publications thus far). But the question that needs to be asked (and is often forgotten) is whether or not its ideas are new, or whether its efficacy is in any way unique. Cognitive reprocessing of traumatic events is a well-established method (Bisson et al., 2007). Careful comparisons show that EMDR is no better than these standard methods (Seidler and Wagner, 2006). It is now generally accepted that eye movements are not a necessary element of the treatment. This method is nothing but old wine in new bottles.

Even so, EMDR has been widely marketed through books and seminars. Like so many of her predecessors, Shapiro is in business and does not work for a university. EMDR remains a product with brand recognition. It may sometimes help people, even if it offers little that is new.

The second example of a fad, recovered memory therapy, presents a more tragic and disturbing story (McHugh, 2008). Since the time of Freud, many therapies have assumed that adult problems are rooted in childhood experiences, and that some of the memories of these events have been "repressed". Repression must count as one of the least helpful ideas in psychotherapy, since it is not supported by research data (McNally, 2003). Moreover, while childhood experiences have some effect on adult life, resilience is ubiquitous, and traumas do not shape adult life in any predictable way (Paris, 2000).

No one has ever convincingly demonstrated that repression actually exists (Holmes, 1990; Schachter, 1996). In addition, memory is *not* a video recorder: most life events are not remembered, and one does not need to invoke repression to account for gaps in memory. Traumatic events are not usually forgotten, but are more likely to stick painfully in memory. It is also not that difficult to implant false memories of trauma (Loftus and Davis, 2006).

How then did educated people and professionals come to believe in such an unscientific theory? In the 1980s and 1990s, the culture supported it (Ofshe and Watters, 1994). Society had seen major changes in family roles and structures. Parents, even when they need two incomes (and value a woman's right to work), were anxious about putting their children in day care with strangers. "Paranoid parenting" (Furedi, 2008) created a kind of "group psychosis" in which people began to imagine that day care centers were hotbeds of child abuse. Caregivers were accused of abusing children (on highly dubious evidence), and several workers were sent to prison in high-profile cases. For a while, providing day care became a risky occupation.

In an influential book, a feminist psychiatrist, Judith Herman (1992), claimed that child abuse is *usually* forgotten. This proposal contradicts the clinical features of PTSD (in which memories flash back painfully and uncontrollably) and flies in the face of what is now known about the psychology of memory. Research shows that memories are continuously reconstructed and retold in the light of further experiences (McNally, 2003). And most life events are permanently forgotten. If that were not so, our brains would become terminally cluttered. I am reminded of an old computer I owned which would warn me "hard disk is full" if I tried to save every single document. Although computers now have much larger amounts of data storage, the brain is selective, keeping memories it needs while discarding those it does not.

Repression was a dramatic idea. Many novels and several Hollywood movies (from Hitchock's from Hitchcock's classic *Suspicion* to the later film *Ordinary People*) have used it as a plot device. Discovering a secret makes for a good story. Ellen Bass and Laura Davis, two teachers who decided to be psychotherapists, published *The Courage to Heal*, a book that eventually sold a million copies (Bass and Davis, 1988). They told troubled women that failing to remember child abuse is proof that it *must* have happened. It proposed that therapy can recover these repressed memories. But detailed descriptions of such therapeutic procedures demonstrate that their methods of recovering memories are suggestive to the point of being coercive (McNally, 2003).

Recovered memory methods were widely used in patients with the diagnosis of multiple personality disorder (now renamed dissociative identity disorder, or DID). While a few rare cases of DID were described in the past, they suddenly became common when therapists wrote about them, and when the media took them up (McHugh, 2008).

There is good reason to believe that most "multiples" were created by suggestive therapy techniques. In a famous example, the patient who inspired the best-selling book *Sibyl* (Schreiber, 1973) told a substitute therapist that she was willing to create multiple personalities if he was interested, but would leave them at home if he was not (Pope, 1997; Rieber, 2006). *Sibyl*, her therapist Cornelia Wilbur, and the author Flora Reta Schreiber, concocted a fiction that made them wealthy (Nathan, 2011).

Recovered memory therapy went on to create an international scandal. It led to lawsuits against therapists from accused parents and brought shame on the profession of psychotherapy. For example, at Rush Presbyterian Hospital, linked to the Department of Psychiatry of the University of Chicago, a physician kept patients on a ward for years encouraging them to manufacture new personalities—while collecting enormous fees (Pendergrast, 1996). In the end, a large settlement had to be paid out by the hospital for tolerating the situation, and the psychiatrist who ran the unit lost his license to practice.

Some years ago, I was invited to speak at a Canadian university about my research on the relationship between child abuse and personality disorders. What I did not know was that the other speaker was a strong believer in recovered memory and that a local community of therapists who treated patients with supposed multiple personality disorder would be turning out for the conference. I discussed the difference between true and false memories of child abuse, noting that reports of satanic ritual abuse were an almost sure sign of false memories, since no one could ever corroborate such stories (in which babies are sacrificed to Satan and ritually eaten). I heard an audible hiss from the audience and realized that I was confronted with true believers who were in no way interested in data.

How does one deal with a malignant fad? Along with others (McNally, 2003; McHugh, 2008), I chose to write scientific articles to counter the recovered memory movement. While these ideas were initially embraced by media figures, with time, they eventually went into decline—as one might have expected with a fad. Therapists came to realize that memory is reconstructed and influenced by states of mind and functioning in the present. And attempts to "recover" memories are particularly likely to produce fabrications.

There is a larger moral of the story. While this troubled period in the history of psychotherapy has crested and receded, it has demonstrated how treatment can sometimes be dangerous (Lilienfeld et al., 2001). Patients suffered from bad therapy, and innocent people even went to prison (Ofshe and Watters, 1994). This debacle demonstrates the dangers of unscientific treatment, supported by the media.

In summary, psychotherapy, which should be based on science, can be infected by pseudoscience. This is what can happen when schools trump data, and when drama takes precedence over sober facts. And this is one of the reasons why bad therapy can cause harm.

Many of the more faddish forms of psychotherapy have taken on characteristics that strongly resemble religious beliefs. Filling a niche left by the decline of religion, they turned into a quasi-religious movement in their own right (Epstein, 2006). One example is Erhard Seminars Training (EST; Pressman, 1993). Developed by an untrained businessman (Jack Rosenberg, who later changed his name to Werner Erhard), EST was a group psychotherapy that claimed to promote success and life skills. Erhard based his method on a wide range of sources, including Zen Buddhism, scientology, and encounter groups.

EST meetings were held in large groups and were more like religious revival meetings than psychotherapy. (However, evangelists do not usually charge large sums for church attendance.) These meetings were heavy on enthusiasm and light on content. To this day, it is hard to determine what these seminars were trying to teach. Like Zen, you were just expected to "get it". And needless to say, the amount of research published on EST is precisely zero. The EST fad passed out of the public view following revelations of Erhard's history of tax evasion, as well as his incestuous abuse of his daughters—leading the founder to move to Europe and leave the movement he founded (later called "The Forum") to disciples.

Scientology is an even more dramatic example of how psychotherapy can morph into a religion. Founded by science fiction writer L. Ron Hubbard, it began as a method called "dianetics" (Gardner, 1957). Rather like earlier versions of psychoanalysis (and even more like recovered memory methods), dianetics proposed that psychological problems result from "engrams" (traumatic memories), some of which were supposed to derive from intra-uterine life.

As a pseudoscience, scientology might well have died a natural death. But Hubbard turned it into a formal religion registered with the government (Kent, 2001). While that decision was originally made for tax purposes, the creation of a Church of Scientology led to an expansion of the movement, followed by the recruitment of a number of celebrities. One can hardly say that this trajectory has been blunted, even decades after the death of Hubbard.

It goes without saying that science was never part of Scientology. In fact, the movement has been famously hostile to medical science, and to psychiatry in particular. Members of the cult promote anti-psychiatric views, using celebrity acolytes to attack the treatment of mental illness. Scientology has also for some years organized demonstrations, targeting TV audiences, at the annual spring meeting of the American Psychiatric Association. It is a truly malignant cult.

The Babel of psychotherapy

The therapy scene is a vast Babel of theories and methods. Decades ago, Kovel (1976) wrote a book listing several hundred "name-brand" treatments. Since then hundreds more have appeared. Many are associated with a three-letter acronym—a marketing device that makes a method easy to remember.

Schools of thought multiply endlessly because money is involved. Ideas developed by charismatic therapists are promoted using a business model. While I have nothing in principle against capitalism, it is not the ideal way to provide human services.

Consumers of psychotherapy must be baffled by these choices. How can they decide whether to seek the services of a more reputable therapy, or something more radical or "new age"? And even among the reputable methods, how to choose? Each competes for a market niche, but while rhetoric is thick, facts are thin.

Imagine if patients who needed surgery had to choose among practitioners using entirely different methods. That is the situation for patients seeking psychotherapy. And there is no regulation. While clinical psychologists and other mental health professionals have to demonstrate that they are qualified, the more general term "psychotherapist" has not corresponded to a regulated profession of its own. However, in 2007, the Canadian province of Ontario passed a "Psychotherapy Act" restricting the use of the term to a defined group of mental health professionals.

Not every surgeon operates in exactly the same way, but there is some degree of consensus about what to do and for whom. That is not true for psychotherapy. While there has been some attempt by the American Psychiatric Association and the American Psychological Association to introduce practice guidelines for treatment, they do not have a strong influence on clinicians.

So why have there been so many schools of therapy, rather than one method that more or less everyone agrees on? In some ways, the explanation lies in the nature of modernity. We live in a fragmented world. When it comes to psychotherapy, which can deal with questions about how to live one's life, failure to agree is not very surprising. We do not all go to the same church—or to any church at all. But Babel and chaos do not guide patients to seek the most appropriate form of help.

As Chapter 3 will show, research findings provide support for psychotherapy as well as for a common framework of treatment. If all methods that are effective work in much the same way, there is no good reason to promote competing schools (Norcross and Goldfried, 2005). Each school may have some good ideas. Why not combine them into one, and simply call it "psychotherapy"?

3
Science and Psychotherapy

Psychotherapy can sometimes look more like a business than a scientific procedure. Too often, hype trumps research data and is used to support marketing of a product. Yet even if the world of psychotherapy is a marketplace, empirical evidence should be the final arbiter. When a new treatment is a drug, governments do not allow it to go in the market without strong evidence. These systematic evaluations are applied to the licensing of every form of pharmacological treatment. Talking therapies should be subject to the same kind of regulation.

As recent economic events have dramatically shown, an unregulated market is bad for consumers. The American Psychological Association publishes a list of "empirically supported therapies", but the public is unaware as to what is or is not listed. It is also not clear to the consumer whether a practitioner who claims to be carrying out a particular therapy can be trusted to do so. Once therapists enter practice, no one checks on their outcomes. Regulation would also help to compensate for the tendency for psychotherapies, each of which may have its own name, to become exercises in narcissism for their creators.

In short, psychotherapy must be based on scientific evidence. The movement for evidence-based treatment, originally designed for medical care (Sackett et al., 1997), has now been applied to clinical psychology (Norcoss and Goldfried, 2005). To be fair, the movement has limitations. For example, many surgeries in current use have never been tested in clinical trials. But agreed standards provide a necessary corrective for the tendency for treatments based on "schools of thought". In the hard world of science, rhetoric is not enough—you have to back up your theories with data.

Even so, there is still a large gap between research and practice. Most psychotherapists are psychologists or social workers (with a spattering of psychiatrists). All receive training in how to carry out treatment, but the quality of this education is highly variable (Weissman et al., 2006). No absolute standard exists, and requirements for continuing education once therapists are in practice are loose.

By and large, practitioners have to learn most of what they know on the job. But while some clinical experience is better than none, it is not a sufficient basis for effective practice. You could be doing the same things for years and be wrong the whole time. O'Donnell (1997, p. 27) once defined clinical experience as "making the same mistakes with increasing confidence over an impressive number of years". And while most talking therapies have been based on strong beliefs, belief systems are not to be trusted without evidence to support them.

Let us consider in more detail why clinical experience has limited value. We all see the world through the lens of our preconceptions (Kagan, 1998). Whatever therapists believe, their observations tend to confirm their theories, and patients may even present material in a way that pleases the therapist by confirming their preconceptions (Frank and Frank, 1991). This process is not always obvious, but it creates a *confirmation bias* (Baron, 2000). Therapists focus on certain questions (and propose certain answers) in a way that confirms previously held ideas.

Second, therapists are not the best people to evaluate the efficacy of their own treatment. As providers of services, they are heavily invested in proving that their hard work has yielded results. They may remember successes and forget (or dismiss) failures. Research shows that patients' perceptions of what is happening are much better predictors of outcome than how therapists believe the treatment is going (Gaston et al., 1998).

Third, therapists should not generalize from the small number of patients in their own practice to larger populations. A series of successes in therapy may reflect a good choice of clients, or a run of luck. A *selection bias* arises when one generalizes from atypical samples (Baron, 2000). That is why results need to be confirmed by multiple systematic clinical trials.

In medicine, the first formal clinical trial of any drug treatment (streptomycin for tuberculosis) dates only to the late 1940s. The movement toward evidence-based practice is a relatively recent development in psychiatry, and the application of evidence-based methods to psychotherapy goes back only 40 years (Lambert, 2003).

A turning point occurred 60 years ago when the famous British psychologist Hans Eysenck published an article entitled "The Effects of Psychotherapy", challenging therapists to *prove* that their methods actually worked. Eysenck (1952) argued that although psychological treatment was ubiquitous in the practice of psychology and psychiatry, evidence for its usefulness was slim. Describing results without comparison to a control group cannot prove anything, since equal numbers might have gotten better with no treatment. To demonstrate efficacy, psychotherapy has to show that it produces better results than naturalistic remission over time.

At the time Eysenck's article was published, evidence-based practice was far from standard. Thus, many therapists rejected the challenge out of hand, showing little interest in conducting research that might disprove their beliefs. Few clinicians during that period understood what the minimal standard of proof in science has to be. They thought it sufficient to draw conclusions from clinical experience or on the basis of published case reports. Eysenck was absolutely right to question the conventional wisdom of his time.

Over the next five decades, an enormous scientific literature has been published, in which psychotherapy has been subjected to clinical trials to prove its efficacy, and in which its methods and processes have been examined systematically. Slowly but surely, data emerged to answer all these questions.

What research showed was that while therapy does not always work, some interventions are definitely effective. A vast body of evidence, supported by meta-analyses of randomized controlled trials (RCTs), has shown that talking therapies can be effective for a wide variety of psychological problems (this body of literature is summarized in Lambert, 2003). Results are most consistent for methods (such as Cognitive behavioral therapy (CBT)) that have a strong base in theory and are well structured in practice. Moreover, clinical trials have examined psychotherapy in the same way as researchers assess drugs, randomizing assignment to treatment conditions and comparing outcome to generic support, waiting list, or to no treatment at all. For this reason, it is not likely that talking therapy works mainly through placebo effects or that it is no different from unscientific traditional healing.

Almost all reviews of the scientific evidence have come to this conclusion (Kazdin, 2008; Roth and Fonagy, 2005; Lazar, 2010). It must be acknowledged, however, that everyone does not agree. Some critics of psychotherapy (e.g., Epstein, 1995) are still not convinced that outcome research is strong enough to prove its case and consider it to be at best a placebo. Epstein (2006) also suggested that the belief system supporting the therapy enterprise has become a religion.

What these critiques fail to take into account is the fact that all scientific findings are limited by their methods and their samples. Dawes

(1994), a well-known skeptic in clinical psychology, described how he initially doubted the conclusion that psychotherapy is effective, but was convinced by conducting some comparisons of his own, in which the results of clinical trials that had methodological problems were not very different from those of the most systematic research. Dawes went on to describe himself as a "reformed sinner" who came to support the efficacy of psychotherapy, although he cautioned that the effect size is neither large nor consistent and that we do not understand very well why therapy works.

While criticism of the meta-analyses supporting the efficacy of psychotherapy is largely mistaken, it has performed a service. Research methods can always be improved. The placebo effects of talking therapy must always be factored in when considering outcome. And researchers have, with a few exceptions (Strupp et al., 1977), not given enough attention to the failures of psychotherapy.

Many of the same questions have arisen with drug treatments, particularly concerning the efficacy of antidepressants. Meta-analyses of clinical trials have shown that these drugs are over-rated and that they do not always outperform placebos (Kirsch et al., 2008). Nonetheless, antidepressants are far from useless and play a key role in the treatment of severe depression.

Similarly, psychotherapy, presented as a cure-all in the past, retains a useful role in practice, particularly for patients in whom drug treatment is not effective. The best track record for talking therapy is in mild to moderate cases of anxiety and depression (Lambert, 2003). While some patients get better on their own, psychotherapy consistently produces better results than natural remission. In addition, specific forms of therapy have now been shown to be effective for at least some patients with severe disorders that are not very amenable to drug treatment: substance abuse (Miller and Rolnick, 2002), and borderline personality disorder (Paris, 2008b).

A caution: these findings do *not* show that psychotherapy is uniformly or predictably efficacious. Moreover, criticism is justified when one considers how much clinical practice consists of non-evidence-based methods that provide little more than simple support.

Psychotherapy should also not be allowed to go on for too long. There is little empirical support for therapies that last more than six months: most evidence for efficacy comes from research on shorter-term treatment. The practice of keeping patients in talking therapy for years says more about the problems of modern culture than about the validity of the procedure. This having been said, talking therapy that is well focused, well planned, systematically carried out, and time-limited is a scientifically valid procedure that helps many patients.

Although a great deal of science has been applied to psychotherapy, clinical practice continues to be largely based on belief systems (Frazier et al., 2008). Adopting the principles of evidence-based treatment would require a major cultural change among therapists. Even now, the process has just begun. Clinicians may not even want to apply methods supported by research, if it is easier to continue applying what they already think they know. Moreover, very few practitioners read academic journals on a regular basis. (They are more likely to depend on conferences and workshop presentations.)

Reviewing the status of clinical psychology 20 years ago, the American psychology professor Robyn Dawes (1994) concluded that an attempt to upgrade the field by requiring therapists to obtain a PhD had not succeeded. There are still Master's level psychologists, but the expectation is more and more for a doctorate. The idea behind requiring a PhD was to create a new generation of research practitioners with experience in clinical investigation, who would conduct empirically based treatment. This admirable idea turned out to be an almost complete failure.

Dawes observed that clinical psychologists go to graduate school, where they are required to carry out a research project of some kind. But many of these projects are of limited validity, and most are never published. Moreover, there is no assurance that psychologists will become acculturated to a scientific perspective once they enter practice, as most graduates have no further involvement with research. In fact, clinicians with PhDs (whose doctorates give a false impression of science) have sponsored some of the most bizarre developments in psychotherapy. One can be a member of the American Psychological Association, and attend its annual meetings, without having anything that resembles an empirical approach to practice.

Although psychologists and social workers are the most common providers of psychotherapy, a recent survey (Weissman et al., 2006) found that psychiatrists, because of their medical education, receive the best training in evidence-based practice—even better than psychologists. (Whether or not psychiatrists use that training in their daily work is another question.) Unfortunately, most medical specialists, in spite of their training, do not consider psychotherapy to be a central part of their work (Paris, 2008a). Social workers, who have the weakest scientific training, end up doing much of the heavy lifting.

Evidence-based practice should be a dominant paradigm for psychiatry and clinical psychology, and both the American Psychiatric and

American Psychological Association publish guidelines for treating various groups of patients, largely based on the results of clinical trials (Chambless and Hollon, 1998). But practitioners have been slow to adopt these recommendations (or even to read them). This failure to observe guidelines is not unique to therapists (most physicians practice medicine in their own way).

Evidence-based practice has also been linked with a movement to integrate all forms of psychotherapy (Norcross and Goldfried, 2005). The idea is to stop promoting brand names, to use one method of therapy (with variations) for most patients, and to apply scientific procedures to test the value of each of these variations. This point of view is consistent with research findings that show that most therapies, whatever their names, work much in the same way (Wampold, 2001).

Since clinicians often have strong allegiances to one method or another, consumers of psychotherapy need to be protected by formal regulatory mechanisms. In the United States, the Food and Drug Administration would not allow sub-par foods or ineffective drugs to go in the market. Psychotherapy should be regulated in the same way. At present, there is not even any overall control over the use of the word *psychotherapy* (Chambless and Hollon, 1998). It remains possible for almost anyone to hang out the proverbial shingle and simply declare oneself as a therapist (or "counselor"). Not every psychologist or social worker has a systematic training, and the problem is even worse for those who simply *claim* to be therapists. The consumer has no guarantee that evidence-based methods will be offered.

Thus while in principle, nothing prevents psychotherapy from being scientific, there is no way of ensuring that services are up to the standard. Like the financial market, clinical practice may only be placed under regulation when disasters happen.

What science tells us about psychotherapy

The "bible" of psychotherapy research is the *Handbook of Psychotherapy and Behavior Change,* first published in 1978, edited by Allen Bergin and Sol Garfield, and revised about every seven years. The fifth edition of the handbook (Lambert, 2003) followed the same tradition, summarizing an enormous body of data. A sixth edition, also edited by Michael Lambert of Brigham Young University, is expected in 2013.

The weight of evidence leaves little doubt that psychotherapy is more effective, at least for most patients, than naturalistic recovery without treatment. As a 1980 book, based on the results of a large-scale meta-analysis of hundreds of published studies, *The Benefits of Psychotherapy* concluded that "Psychotherapy benefits people of all ages as reliably as school educates them, medicine cures them, or business turns a profit" (Smith et al., 1980, p. 10). The overall effect can be calculated in meta-analyses (a technique for combining the results of many studies to determine the size of a relationship). The effect size, at least half a standard deviation, is clinically significant (Smith et al., 1980). If one were measuring intelligence, such a difference would correspond to raising IQ by ten points. Later meta-analyses have not changed this verdict (Lambert, 2003).

But not everyone gets educated (or cured), and business does not always turn a profit. Not everyone benefits from psychotherapy, and some waste years in futile treatment. Moreover, findings based on randomized clinical trials do not prove that any and all methods are good for any and all patients. Many people are better off without therapy. And if treatment *is* recommended, practitioners need to tailor approaches for different symptoms—what helps a client with anxiety may not be suitable for one with substance abuse.

There are two complementary ways to study the effects of psychotherapy. One is *effectiveness* research, the study of treatment in "naturalistic" populations (real clinical settings where patients are not excluded because of unsuitability for a clinical trial). An example was a large-scale survey conducted by the American psychologist Martin Seligman, using data obtained from thousands of readers of the magazine *Consumer Reports* (Seligman, 1995). This research simply asked subjects to describe their experiences with psychotherapy and the extent to which they had benefited from it.

There is value in studying psychotherapy in the real world rather than in an experiment. However, the problem with effectiveness research is that it fails to use a control group. Would patients have gotten well with a different type of treatment, with less treatment, or with no treatment at all? The *Consumer Reports* survey, which had no controls, could not answer those questions. We also do not know whether the readers of that magazine (highly educated, committed to quality, and self-selected by answering the survey) are in any way representative of the larger population of patients.

The second, and more scientifically rigorous, approach to studying psychotherapy is to examine its effects in clinical trials, in much the same way as we test drugs. This is called *efficacy* research, the study of treatment using RCTs. Patients are randomly assigned to options such as treatment versus no treatment, two different treatments, or treatment versus minimal support. The main problem in interpreting RCTs lies in determining whether results in research samples generalize to patients seen in practice. People who enter clinical trials and agree to be randomized may not resemble the patients whom therapists see.

Efficacy and effectiveness research are complementary and offer a kind of trade-off (Hogarty et al., 1997). Efficacy is based on a controlled experiment but may not be applicable to real patients; effectiveness is based on real-world data, but lack of controls makes conclusions uncertain. In either method, there has to be a standard way to measure outcome. One can rate changes in symptoms, improvements in functioning in work and relationships, or look at overall quality of life.

A few studies have compared psychotherapy with medication. Drugs are essential for more severe disorders, such as schizophrenia, melancholic depression, or bipolar disorder. Yet even in psychotic patients, psychotherapy can add real value to medication regimes (Tarrier, 2005). That is why the National Health Service in the UK has been hiring more psychologists to conduct CBT. On the other hand, drugs are not very effective for common symptoms such as milder depression (Kirsch et al., 2008). This is where psychotherapy can play a crucial role.

How psychotherapy works

If talking therapy sometimes helps but sometimes fails, we need to understand the mechanisms behind the process. The American psychiatrist and psychologist Jerome Frank was one of the great pioneers of psychotherapy research. Frank, a medical specialist with a PhD in psychology, had a strong commitment to science at a time when therapy was based entirely on clinical opinion. In most ways, he was far ahead of his time.

Frank's classic book on the social roots of psychotherapy argued that talking therapy helps people in much the same way as traditional religion. As Frank and Frank (1991) put it (p. 62), "the core of the effectiveness of methods of religious and magical healing seems to lie in their ability to arouse hope of capitalizing on the patient's dependency on others." As the authors went on to say (pp. 333–334): "faith may be a specific antidote for demoralization, while the mobilization of expectant trust by whatever means may be as much an etiological remedy as penicillin for pneumonia" (p. 132). They hypothesized that patients who are more suggestible are more likely to accept socially defined healing and concluded: "Our survey has suggested that much, if not all, of the effectiveness of different forms of psychotherapy may be due to those features that all have in common" (p. 232).

Much of what can be said about psychotherapy today is an epilogue to the ideas of Jerome Frank. Research over the last 50 years has consistently supported his concept of the universal elements of healing. Frank's book *Persuasion and Healing,* first published in 1962 and then in revised editions (Frank and Frank, 1991), developed a model that explains why so many different types of therapies work, independent of the theories underlying the methods. Frank saw psychotherapy as a process in which patients arrive demoralized and hopeless but improve by regaining morale and hope. Thus, psychotherapy is not just a technical procedure, but a healing relationship. Frank's conclusion was that the theories behind therapy tend to be irrelevant, as long as that process is set into motion. He suggested that almost any theory might do, as long as the patient is willing to accept it. As Frank pointed out, traditional and faith healers, too, have had a fair record of success in managing psychological symptoms.

The most striking confirmation for Frank's ideas has come from *comparative trials* of psychotherapy. In that research, researchers randomly assign patients to different methods to determine if one is better than another. What consistently emerges from the data is that no particular form of treatment is more effective than any other.

A 1936 paper by the American psychology professor Saul Rosenzweig was the first to establish the principle (Duncan, 2002). Referring to the absence of differences in the outcome of various forms of psychotherapy, Rosenzweig, citing Lewis Carroll's *Alice in Wonderland* (in which the dodo declares after a race that everyone has won and all shall have prizes), described these results wittily as a "dodo bird" verdict. Decades later, the American psychologist Lester Luborsky published a much-quoted paper entitled *"Comparative Studies of Psychotherapy: Is It True That Everyone Has Won and All Shall Have Prizes?"* (Luborsky et al., 1975). Reviewing all existing comparative trials, the clear conclusion was that Rosenzweig was still right on the mark.

Recent systematic reviews continue to support the dodo bird verdict. Bruce Wampold, a psychologist at the University of Wisconsin, reviewed this subject in great depth ten years ago (Wampold, 2001). When researchers compare one therapy to another, differences in efficacy hardly ever emerge. (And even when they do, differences are rarely replicable by researchers who have no allegiance to any one approach.) These findings show that theory and technique are not as crucial as many have believed. Thus, while some therapists are better than others, results do not depend on how experienced they are, whether they are male or female, or on what kind of training they have had (Beutler et al., 2003). The overall skill of a therapist in getting patients engaged in the treatment process is much more important.

Therapeutic skill is, at least in part, a natural talent. That conclusion is supported by research showing that experienced therapists can sometimes be no more effective than novices. In a famous study, Hans Strupp, a leading psychotherapy researcher, carried out a clinical trial intended to demonstrate the importance of technique and experience (Strupp and Hadley, 1979). His research design compared the effectiveness of treatment from experienced therapists with that of "treatment" provided by university professors who had been rated by their students as unusually sympathetic. I remember talking to Strupp at a conference in 1976, as he explained how he hoped to show that experience makes a real difference. But no difference in outcome was found between experienced therapists and non-professionals.

The limitation of this study was that the patients receiving therapy were students in mild distress, who volunteered for a research study—not real patients with severe and diagnosable problems. Even so, other attempts to show effects of experience have yielded weak or unreplicated findings (Beutler et al., 2003). My own research group (Propst et al., 1994) was unable to find any difference in the results of brief therapy conducted by medical students with no experience, family practice residents with very limited experience, psychiatric residents with more experience, or staff psychiatrists with many years of experience. The fact that experience is not a strong predictor of outcome suggests that therapeutic skill is a talent—even if teaching can make a talented trainee better.

The importance of talent also helps to explain why common factors (also called "non-specific factors") remain the best predictors of outcome in therapy (Wampold, 2001; Hubble et al., 1999; Miller and Duncan, 1997). The most important common factor is the quality of the *therapeutic alliance* between the therapist and the patient. Therapeutic skills depend on empathy—the ability to connect with patients. A large body of research confirms that when measures of the therapeutic alliance are administered, even after only a few sessions of therapy, they consistently predict whether treatment will be successful (Luborsky and Luborsky, 2006).

That is also what Strupp et al. (1969) found when a group of patients were asked what they got out of therapy. Most said they could not even remember what they had talked about—it was the *process* that felt good.

In another study in which therapists themselves were asked about their experiences as psychotherapy patients (Buckley et al., 1981), the results were much the same.

These observations raise the question of whether psychotherapy is only "the purchase of friendship" (Schofield, 1964). In fact, research shows that "befriending" (supportive contact with unpaid but sympathetic volunteers) is an effective treatment for mild depression (Mead et al., 2010). But this kind of intervention is not sufficient for more severe problems. We need to define more precisely the elements that make common factors predictably effective.

Carl Rogers was an American psychologist who developed a method called "client-centered therapy" (Rogers, 1951). This treatment had little to do with psychoanalysis, but depended on a theory that people get better naturally and that therapy serves mainly a catalyst for change. But Rogers' concepts were too simplistic, and his experience was based on the treatment of people with milder problems.

Yet Rogers' research method defined the basic elements that therapists have to provide: *accurate empathy, unconditional positive regard, and genuineness.* These conditions for good therapy are a minimum; they are necessary but not sufficient—therapists need to more than just affirm feelings (Orlinsky et al., 1994). Nevertheless, patients remember the *experience* of being understood in therapy more than they do of understanding their psyche or learning any particular skill. This observation is consistent with the conclusion that techniques are less important than therapists think.

In summary, research strongly confirms the ideas of Jerome Frank. The data stand in strong contrast to the marketing of specific methods. Frank had emphasized that therapy is a relationship and that psychotherapy provides troubled people with an "expert companion" who understands their distress and guides them out of a morass. Patients tend to agree with that judgment. Instead of telling their friends how brilliant their therapist's comments are, they usually talk about how it feels to have a therapist who understands them.

Which patients benefit from psychotherapy?

Characteristics of patients determine whether the outcome of therapy will be positive or negative. This rich area of research has been summarized in extensive literature reviews (Garfield, 1994; Beutler et al., 2003). Most of the predictors are not very surprising. Patients must accept the framework of talking therapy and must also be ready to work within it.

By and large, the more distressed people are, the more motivated they are for therapy. On the other hand, some have serious symptoms (such as substance abuse) that they fail to see as problems. When treating such patients, therapists should not assume that they want to change their behaviors. A whole sequence of processes has to happen before people become serious about change (Prochaska et al., 1994). Special procedures, termed "motivational interviewing", have been developed to deal with patients who are not yet ready to change their behavior (Miller and Rollnick, 2002). Motivation for change is a complex phenomenon, and it is always important to respect ambivalence about a need for therapy.

Paradoxically, while distress can be motivating, people who are highly dysfunctional are less likely to benefit. This general rule reflects the fact that patients who have strengths (e.g., a good job and friends) have something to lean on when dealing with weaknesses (usually in intimate relationships). Moreover, people who have developed areas of good functioning are intrinsically more resourceful. By and large, those whose functional level is higher before treatment do better than those who are not functioning well at all. In this way, the rich get richer and the poor get poorer.

Diagnosis is not a strong predictor of outcome. This reflects the fact that patients who go into therapy only meet criteria for just a few out of the many possible psychiatric diagnoses. Most patients have a major depression, an anxiety disorder, or a personality disorder. Some have substance abuse or an eating disorder. (Very few patients in talking therapy suffer from schizophrenia or bipolar disorder.) The presence of more than one diagnosis is a measure of severity. The more symptoms you have, the more criteria you will meet for various disorders listed in the Diagnostic and Statistical Manual (DSM). And if you also have substance abuse, your prognosis is even more guarded.

One group of diagnoses, common in clinical practice, strongly influences the outcome of therapy. These are the personality disorders, which can be identified in about half of all patients attending hospital or community clinics (Zimmerman et al., 2008). A diagnosis of a personality disorder, by definition (American Psychiatric Association, 2000), describes long-term impairment of psychosocial functioning. This is the one condition that therapists particularly need to recognize (even if they often don't), since these patients do less well in therapy (Elkin et al., 1989; Newton-Howes et al., 2006), and need specific forms of treatment tailored for their problems (Paris, 2008b). If your relationships with other people are troubled, you are more likely to have problems establishing a connection to a therapist. And people who cannot hold a job may not even show up regularly for sessions.

Some personality disorders are very disabling. The borderline type (my own research interest) is characterized by chronic suicidality, self-harm behaviors, as well as frequent emergency room visits and hospitalizations (Paris, 2008b). Others, like narcissistic personality disorder (to be discussed in Chapter 6), have more subtle (but nonetheless palpable) effects on work and relationships.

Above and beyond the presence of a diagnosable disorder, everyone has a personality, a unique set of traits that influence how we feel, behave, and interact with others. These trait profiles also have effects on functioning (Plomin et al., 2001). As discussed in Chapter 1, one can distinguish an "externalizing" style (Krueger, 1999), that is, a tendency to blame others for their troubles, rather than look inside, and to act out rather than examine inner causes of distress from an "internalizing" style, that is, a tendency to blame themselves, and to withdraw and suffer rather than deal with problems directly. Those with an externalizing style are less suitable for therapy, because they may not be sufficiently self-critical to make use of therapy. In contrast, people with an internalizing style are more likely to seek talking therapy and to benefit from it.

Another way to conceptualize these indicators is by a capacity for "psychological-mindedness" (McCallum and Piper, 1997). This refers to the ability to observe oneself—an essential quality for anyone who hopes to benefit from psychotherapy. Recently, this capacity has been termed *mentalization* (Bateman and Fonagy, 2006), a concept based on the theory of mind. One of the current frontiers of therapy concerns developing skills of self-observation, called "mindfulness" (Segal et al., 2002).

Culture also affects suitability for psychotherapy. People adhering to non-Western cultures, immigrants, and people with limited education do somewhat less well in therapy (Kirmayer, 2004). These differences reflect cultural influences, in that distress may be expressed in physical rather than in psychological symptoms (Kleinman, 1988). A large body of research suggests that patients who are not acculturated to modern values are more likely to have more concrete symptoms such as pain or fatigue, rather than abstract mental states such as anxiety or depression (Kirmayer, 2007).

Since no single factor is a strong predictor of outcome, the effects of psychotherapy can be surprising. As one senior researcher noted, the existing data is not much better than clinical intuition in deciding which patients to treat and how to treat them (Garfield, 1994). Experienced psychotherapists can use that intuition to decide who they are most likely to help.

Process and technique

The focus of *process research* in psychotherapy is to identify mechanisms of change as therapy unfolds. Orlinsky et al. (1994) examined research on over 50 different variables describing the process of psychotherapy in relation to outcome. Once again, "non-specific" factors emerged as most important. What helps most patients (in all forms of psychotherapy) is: (1) a well-defined contract; (2) a strong alliance; (3) encouragement of openness; and (4) a focus on current life problems and relationships.

Many specific interventions in therapy, long thought to be crucial for outcome, have *not* been shown to be dramatically effective. For example, no consistent data show that "interpretations" linking present difficulties to childhood experiences are effective, or that discussing "transference" (when patients repeat past problems in their relationship to the therapist) makes a difference. These methods are still being used (Hoglend et al., 2008) but are problematic. One study (Ogrodniczuk et al., 1999) found that the more the therapist suggested that problems in the therapeutic relationship were based on transference, the worse became the outcome. The ideas proposed by Freud about how therapy works have not been confirmed.

CBT aims to maximize common factors, in part by working collaboratively with patients. But it is not clear whether its specific techniques are crucial. It is the overall package that has been shown to be effective. Thus, we do not know whether specific interventions (such as homework to ensure self-observation, exercises to modify negative thoughts, or mindfulness to establish distance from symptoms) are either necessary or sufficient. To answer that question one would have to carry out a "dismantling" strategy in which therapy is pared down, piece by piece—until it stops working (Hunsley and Rumstein-McKean, 1999). But almost no one has funds for such complex research.

What seems to make the most consistent difference in process is the application of a *predictable structure* (Orlinsky et al., 2003). Whether therapists offer interpretations, recommend modifications of thought patterns, or suggest ways to improve relationships, patients do better if there is a clear plan and treatment is not allowed to drift.

The rise of CBT

CBT is currently the most scientific method of psychological treatment. The man who coined the term is Aaron Beck (born in 1921), a psychiatrist who worked for many years at the University of Pennsylvania. Beck, now in his 90s, is one of the few specialists in psychiatry to have won the Lasker Prize, the highest honor in American medicine.

Albert Ellis (2001) developed Rational Emotive Therapy (RET) at around the same time. This method has some similarities to CBT and has stimulated a little research (Lyons and Woods, 1991). But Ellis was more of a showman than a scientist, who showed more interest in popularizing his method and marketing it than in studying it. It is Beck who deserves the credit for developing a scientific therapy with broad clinical applications. Originally trained as a psychoanalyst, but unimpressed with results, Beck developed an approach that challenges belief systems and cognitive errors (particularly negative feelings about future, self, and the world) that make people anxious and depressed. Unlike Freud, Beck conducted rigorous clinical trials to show that his methods worked, and positive results have been consistently confirmed (Beck, 1986).

The development of CBT was a turning point in the history of talking therapy, creating a culture in which ideas were empirically tested and updated on the basis of clinical trials. CBT has had an enormous impact, creating a "tool box" to deal with many clinical pictures.

Earlier, the British psychologist Hans Eysenck (1916–97), along with the South African-born American psychiatrist Joseph Wolpe (1915–97), had developed a method called behavior therapy (BT), mainly designed to treat anxiety. Its methods focused on exposure to feared stimuli along with relaxation techniques (systematic desensitization and reciprocal inhibition). Behavior therapists considered symptoms to be learned responses that could be unlearned with the proper training. For many years BT was the main alternative to psychoanalysis (Sundberg, 2001). But BT suffered from its lack of interest in the mind. Behaviorists saw the brain as nothing but a "black box" and thought that the only valid (i.e., measurable) phenomena are stimulus and response. These simplistic ideas made BT unsuitable for the management of depression, in which the main problem lies in mood and thought (not behavior). Today these methods have been folded into the practice of CBT.

In summary, Beck brought the mind back into therapy, linked research to practice, and created a new culture, in which science was more important than salesmanship. Research data has also helped to refine CBT, which now uses a broader range of techniques used for a wider range of clinical problems, including psychosis (Turkington et al., 2006) as well as personality disorders (Linehan, 1993). CBT has a toolkit filled with techniques that can be applied to almost any set of symptoms. And it continues to develop in new directions, as shown by the current interest in mindfulness, emotion regulation, and acceptance strategies (Hofmann et al., 2010).

CBT has greatly impressed mental health professionals. As hundreds of research papers demonstrated its efficacy, it rapidly filled the niches previously occupied by older therapies. Unlike psychoanalysis, CBT does not spend years reviewing a patient's childhood. CBT therapists believe that rather than focusing on personal histories, patients need to put the past behind them and address problems in the present. Doing so helps to shorten the duration of treatment. Another strength is the presence of a clear structure and an agreed plan. Finally, a built-in feedback system encourages patients to comment on whether they feel helped at the end of every session.

Is CBT also a "school"? Yes and no. Although it is an evidence-based form of psychotherapy whose efficacy has been proven in clinical trials, the field has not always shown interest in adapting methods developed by therapists of other persuasions. CBT tends to be a world unto itself, applying its methods to almost any psychological problem. It would benefit from integrating the best ideas of other therapists.

We do not know exactly how CBT works. It may be particularly good at tapping into the common factors that lie behind all effective treatment. Yet while CBT has done a better job at documenting its effectiveness, in head-to-head comparisons with other methods, it is not necessarily superior (Elkin et al., 1989).

Interpersonal therapy (IPT; Weissman and Klerman, 1993) is the other main evidence-based form of psychological treatment, developed by the late American psychiatrist (and ex-psychoanalyst) Gerald Klerman, and his epidemiologist wife, Myrna Weissman. Like CBT, IPT focuses on the present and is brief and practical. It also has generated a fair amount of research: one large-scale clinical trial in depression (Elkin et al., 1989) found its efficacy equal to that of CBT.

IPT does not have an elaborate theory, and it differs from CBT in that it uses few specific technical devices. The focus is on the patient's current intimate relations and why they are not working. IPT might be seen as a variant of psychodynamic therapy that does not focus on the past. It is based on the principle that symptoms can arise due to failures of communication in important relationships. IPT has not had the same wide application as CBT, but overlaps between these two approaches are notable, since both work to help patients reframe problems. IPT and CBT can be viewed as variants of the same approach.

One psychotherapy, based on science

A scientific approach to psychotherapy would greatly change the way the field looks today. All schools would disappear. There would only be *one* psychotherapy—not hundreds. Its methods would be based on research findings, not on business models or on the narcissism of therapists who want their names to be remembered.

This may be an impossible dream, but for it to happen, psychological treatment would have to develop the same relationship to academia that drug therapy has with academic psychiatry. Of course, that does not mean mental health care should be corrupted in the way psychiatry has been by the pharmaceutical industry (Healy, 2002). In any case, since profits from psychotherapy go to authors of books, the same problem does not arise. The crucial point is that therapy has to be evidence-based, and that allegiance to any particular method should not be based on entrepreneurship and guild membership. As is becoming more and more the case in medicine, clinical practice should be rooted in research findings.

In addition, the nature of psychotherapy research needs to change. Instead of studying treatment packages as a whole, one could dismantle therapies and identify their crucial elements. Doing so would help to develop a single form of treatment, with enhanced "boutique variations", that is, interventions designed to deal with specific problems. The failure to find specific elements in therapy supports this idea. However researchers could help us to become more specific about non-specifics. If common factors are so powerful, we should identify them more precisely and find a way to optimize them.

Second, therapies should take into account the nature of patient groups. For example, in my own area of interest (patients with borderline personality disorder), methods designed for these unusually troubled people are consistently superior to standard, one-size-fits-all therapy (Paris, 2008b).

Third, treatment goes better when it has a plan. Many patients I see in consultation tell me they attended psychotherapy sessions for many months, but can only remember reporting the events of the previous week. In the absence of a focus, they do not learn much that is useful. This is the proverbial "hand-holding". The success of therapies supported by research is partly due to their having a definable structure. In contrast, unplanned therapy tends to drift.

Finally, while skill in therapy can be measured, it remains a talent. Research suggests that some practitioners are indeed "naturals", while others have to be taught how to conduct therapy, and some people are best advised to stay away from this kind of work. Thus, however much therapy comes to be based on science, day-to-day practice will always be something of an art.

4
Why People Seek Psychotherapy

While many suffer from psychological symptoms, only a minority of the population ever seeks psychotherapy. These days there is doubt about the value of talking about problems: many prefer to take medication, and some resist going for help to any professional. To understand why this happens, let us look at who needs treatment, what makes people open to talking therapy, and what determines access to these services.

Who needs treatment?

Over the course of a lifetime, half of the population of the United States will meet criteria for the diagnosis of at least one mental disorder, as defined by the current diagnostic system (Kessler et al., 2005a). Yet only about 30% of these potential patients obtain professional help (Howard et al., 1996; Olfson et al., 2002; Kessler et al., 2005b). And of those who do, less than half go to a mental health practitioner. The rest consult family doctors, who are most likely to prescribe an antidepressant (and less likely to make a referral for psychotherapy). In any given year, while about a third of the population meets criteria for a mental disorder, only 3% enter *any* kind of talking therapy (Olfson et al., 2002; Olfson and Marcus, 2010).

But is this really a problem? The current diagnostic system in psychiatry, particularly the American Psychiatric Association's series of *Diagnostic and Statistical Manuals* (DSM), is at best a rough and ready way of describing mental illness. The DSM system does a reasonably good job of defining severe disorders (psychosis and melancholia), but a poor job of describing the common problems (anxiety and mild depression) that everyone experiences from time to time. The system has a very unfortunate tendency to pathologize normal human experiences. It has to be taken with a large grain of salt.

Epidemiological surveys, based on the DSM system, give the mistaken impression that mental illness is highly prevalent and almost ubiquitous, so that people should be encouraged to seek treatment. Consumers do not agree and often prefer to manage minor problems on their own. One large-scale survey (Mojtabai et al., 2010) showed that the most common reason for *not* going for help was the feeling that one could (and should) handle life problems without professional assistance.

By and large, the conclusion that large numbers of people have mental disorders of some kind is an artifact of an over-inclusive classification system. The modern world medicalizes human suffering and turns life's vicissitudes into psychiatric diagnoses. Many people who meet criteria for a DSM diagnosis are not disabled. The categories used to define mental disorders fail to make a distinction between severe illness and what Freud called "ordinary human unhappiness".

The standard guide to mental illness used by clinicians is the *Diagnostic Manual for Mental Disorders, fourth edition, Text Revision* (DSM-IV-TR; American Psychiatric Association, 2000). DSM-5 will be published in 2013, and most elements of the previous edition will remain. Hardly any of its categories have been validated in the same way as medical illnesses. Moreover, the manual describes a very wide range of disorders, some of which are probably normal variants. Of the over 400 categories listed in the 900 pages of DSM-IV-TR (American Psychiatric Association, 2000) many are not medical diagnoses, but patterns of symptoms or behaviors that make people unhappy. This situation will not change with the publication of DSM-5. These "problems in living" include mild depression or anxiety, milder degrees of substance abuse, and less severe personality disorders. While such problems should not be dismissed, they need not be thought of as *illnesses*. While the common cold can be considered as much of a disease as pneumonia, it does not require the same aggressive treatment. A good example is the problem of separating clinical depression from sadness (Horwitz and Wakefield, 2007). Many depressive episodes are a normal response to losses and disappointments. In the past, few would have dreamt of seeking help for situations that would make anyone unhappy. In this context, people with milder symptoms are right to wait until they feel better.

In any case, uncertain access to mental health services makes the option impractical, either because people are not insured, or because few clinicians practice in their area. In spite of these barriers, rates for treatment of mental disorders in the United States have been gradually going up, from 20% in 1990 to 33% in 2003 (Kessler et al., 2005b). Gradually, more people are getting professional care for psychological problems. And at least some of that treatment involves psychotherapy.

Who seeks talking therapy?

Research on the characteristics, both psychological and demographic, of patients who seek psychotherapy has shown who is likely to seek this form of treatment (Clarkin and Levy, 2003). The most comprehensive study was a 1997 survey by a group of researchers from Columbia University that examined access to out-patient psychotherapy in a national sample (Olfson et al., 2002).

Four findings were particularly striking. First, women are more likely to seek help than men: about two-thirds of patients in psychotherapy are female. Second, younger people seek therapy more often than older people, the highest rate being among adults between 25 and 54. Third, fewer patients from lower socioeconomic or immigrant groups seek therapy, while most people in treatment are white. Fourth, psychotherapy is practiced more often in large cities than in rural areas.

The researchers compared these results to a previous study from 1987, allowing them to examine trends over time. They noted a decline in the use of long-term therapy in favor of short-term therapy. They also found that poor people have more access than had been the case ten years earlier—which may account for some of the increase in overall levels of use.

Surprisingly, two-thirds of all talking therapy in the 1997 survey was conducted by physicians (mostly psychiatrists). Yet, as shown by a later survey by the same research group, psychiatrists carry out less and less formal psychotherapy (Mojtabai and Olfson, 2008). The most likely explanation is that the original study did not examine in sufficient detail what was meant by "psychotherapy". Psychiatrists who prescribe medication may describe brief chats with patients as if they were formal therapy—because insurance pays them a bit more than for a simple medication check.

In summary, those who seek psychotherapy are an identifiable minority within a population of potential patients. Most people who suffer from problems either take medication or muddle through. But can those who seek talking therapy find it?

Access to psychotherapy

Access to psychotherapy determines how much it is used. This is a serious problem for the rational distribution of mental health services. Psychological treatment costs money—more (at least in the short run) than drugs that can be prescribed for the same problems. It also requires talented and well-trained professionals to administer interventions. And as we will see, there is no guarantee that the quality of treatment meets evidence-based standards.

More people are in talking therapy today than at any other point in history (Olfson et al., 2002). This almost always consists of short-term treatment. Longer therapy is out of reach for most consumers (which may be just as well, since it is not evidence-based). Brief psychotherapy (10–20 sessions) is available in North America—for those who have insurance. The problem for Americans is that if they are unemployed, they won't have insurance. Ironically, although psychotherapy has been around for longer in the United States, and while demand could be high, insurance companies, who see talking as low-tech and old-fashioned, offer very limited coverage. Access is better in the United Kingdom, where the National Health Service has been hiring more psychologists to provide services insured by the government. And in some European countries, almost *all* forms of psychotherapy are fully insured. However access is still limited by the supply of therapists, which rarely meets the demand.

In the United States (and Canada, where I work), even well-trained psychotherapists are marginalized—they can work in institutions, carry out supportive therapy under insurance, or compete for the small market of wealthy (or well-insured) people looking for long-term treatment. There are now fewer therapists who run full-time practices (Olfson et al., 2002), so only a few patients have access to their services. Psychotherapy, when it lasts for more than a short time, is seen as too expensive (Olfson and Pincus, 1994; Olfson et al., 2002). Insurance companies prefer treatment with medication, which they believe (incorrectly) saves them money. The Canadian single-payer health system works well for severely ill patients in hospital or out-patient clinics, but does not cover psychologists outside of hospitals and community clinics. Since psychiatrists do very little of this work, access to psychotherapy is no better than in Canada than in the United States.

In my work as a consultant, I see several hundred people every year referred to a psychiatric clinic by family doctors. Many have been tried on a number of antidepressants without success. I often conclude they have life problems that could benefit from talking. But it is frustrating to find any place to send these people for treatment—unless they are financially comfortable. And even if therapy were better insured, access to quality care will remain limited until there are enough qualified practitioners to provide it.

Insurance companies are right to prefer briefer treatment. In fact, consistent data has shown that making therapy available, even when brief, can actually *save* the health care system money (Gabbard et al., 1997). The reason is that people who have a therapist to talk to are less likely to bother physicians with physical ailments. They also do not end up receiving extensive but useless investigations. (Brain scans and blood tests cost much more than talking.)

It would therefore make sense if there were a broader insurance support of evidence-based psychotherapy, covering at least a reasonable length of treatment based on scientific studies: six months of weekly sessions every year. However, that seems unlikely to happen anytime in the near future. While insurance companies in the United States are now expected by recent legislation to offer "parity", that is, to cover mental illness in the same way as physical disease, nothing forces them to pay for talking therapy.

Moreover, the current model of mental health care delivery offers fragmented treatment. There would be many advantages to integrated multidisciplinary settings, in which psychiatrists, psychologists, social workers, and other professionals work together (Paris, 2008a). But most practitioners of psychotherapy are in private practice and support themselves in a fee-for-service system. They cannot accept uninsured patients who are not in a position to pay their fees, and only a few work on a sliding scale. Finally, clinics in the public sector have never had (and probably never will have) enough trained personnel to provide comprehensive services to patients.

The upshot is that many patients who could benefit from talking therapy either have to go without it or receive psychopharmacology only. Horwitz and Wakefield (2007) noted that an overly broad concept of "major depression" will include anyone who is seriously unhappy for any length of time. All too often, this diagnosis leads to a prescription. Psychotherapy might be more appropriate for such cases. Yet while therapy is effective for patients with many forms of depression, it remains relatively inaccessible. While no mental health professional would consider treating a patient with schizophrenia, bipolar disorder, or severe depression without drugs, these agents are often prescribed for milder conditions for which they are much less effective (Kirsch et al., 2008). Drugs do not cure unhappiness.

Cultural barriers to psychotherapy

Many people who suffer from anxiety or depression have physical (rather than mental) symptoms (Shorter, 1994). A tendency toward "somatization" of distress is notable in traditional societies (Murphy,

1982). For example, a study of Chinese patients found that they rarely complained of depressed mood but more often reported symptoms of weakness (Kleinman, 1988). These differences, while less prominent than they once were, present a major obstacle to talking therapy. It has been said that trying to talk about feelings to a patient who focuses on physical pain or fatigue resembles a situation where two people are speaking different languages.

Even in Western society, "somatization" of depression is the norm (Kirmayer and Robbins, 1991). It is Western culture, not traditional societies, that is unusual: modern patients have been described as "psychologizing" suffering (Ryder et al., 2008). To describe a change in mood (rather than bodily symptoms), a patient must have a modern concept of the self (Kirmayer, 2004). That implies a sense of what one normally feels, compared with one's current mental state.

Psychotherapists expect their clients to see problems as psychological. This means they must have a capacity to introspect, and they may even (in the case of cognitive behavioral therapy) be required to do homework. People from other cultures have little experience in thinking and acting in that way and have difficulty in meeting these expectations. They expect practitioners to provide authoritative answers to problems, as well as medicines to relieve symptoms.

While much effort has gone into making psychotherapy culturally appropriate (Tseng, 1999), applicability is limited by the individualistic assumptions that characterize modern society. The concept of the individual that underlies the therapeutic enterprise is not generally held in cultures outside the Western world, many of which see a person as part and parcel of a social network (Kleinman, 1988; Kirmayer, 2007). In many cultures, going to a stranger and complaining about the behavior of one's closest relatives would be simply out of the question.

Some decades ago, I treated university students from Hong Kong who felt lonely studying abroad (particularly in the cold climate of Canada). But since these students came from a traditional Chinese culture, they were expected to fulfill their families' expectations, and were not allowed to express distress about their situation. I spent a number of frustrating hours trying (unsuccessfully) to get these students to talk. If I were to see the same patients today, I would no doubt take a different approach. Yet as modern values have become globalized, and as cultures are less different, this scenario is a little less common. Some of the same students might now be able to say, "I am depressed".

Therapists should not assume that their patients share the individualistic values of the modern world. Cultural sensitivity is becoming increasingly important in a time of high levels of immigration, and many patients either adhere to other cultures or are in a process of acculturation (Nisbett, 2003). To work with people from other cultures, a therapist has to understand and respect their values. Also, when conducting therapy with the children of immigrants, who have become acculturated while growing up in Western culture, therapists should be aware that these patients can be torn between the forces of tradition and modernity.

I learned these principles working with families in a multi-ethnic clinic. In important ways, family structure is different in other cultures (McGoldrick et al., 2005). The approach to family therapy that I was taught as a psychiatric resident was based on the assumption that treatment should aim to repair faulty communication within the family group. Therapists encouraged a democratic atmosphere: while parents have the last word, children can talk back. In other words, everybody was expected to act like an American.

That approach might work with people who have individualistic values and who accept that children could be (and should be) different from their parents. But it proved disastrous in families whose cultures were traditional and patriarchal. If I challenged the authority of the father, I might never see the family again.

Patriarchy is common in traditional societies (Goldberg, 1973). And there is no evidence that patriarchal values, whether we agree with them or not, are incompatible in any essential way with mental health. The idea that every child should become unique and individual—whatever parents think—is just as cultural as the idea that "Father knows best".

Another example of the interface of culture and therapy in families is the concept of "enmeshment". Family therapists (e.g., Minuchin, 1974) have used that term to describe an inability of young people to separate from their family of origin, a problem believed to be the source of a variety of symptoms. Actually the idea that children should "individuate" and make their own choices in life is rooted in modern values and is not held by all patients (Kirmayer, 2004). For example, there is nothing pathological about adult children living with their parents. Many immigrant families expect children to stay home until they marry. Some cultures arrange marriages for the next generation. There is nothing intrinsically wrong with these options. In modern society, being close to or dependent on one's parents is frowned upon. Modern people also frown upon the idea (common in traditional cultures) that even after marriage, one should continue to give priority to one's parents and siblings. Therapists should not impose cultural agendas and call that "mental health".

Only modern societies promote the level of individuation that many psychotherapists believe to be necessary and normal. In many ways, contemporary cultural values are *anti-family*. Society at large undermines the judgment of parents and frightens them about the consequences of doing what they feel is right for their children (Furedi, 2008). We expect people to form stronger attachments to intimate partners and friends than to family members. People who continue to rely on their parents and siblings may even be considered immature. Yet people become alienated and distressed when they lack family support. As Robert Frost put it in his poem, *The Death of the Hired Man*, "Home is the place where, when you have to go there, they have to take you in."

Therapists also need to know that specific values held by cultural groups can conflict with the modern consensus. For example, I have had experience treating gay patients from parts of the world (China and Latin America), where most people consider homosexuality to be immoral. Whereas a person born in Western society can be validated for consolidating a gay identity, families from these cultures may never accept that choice.

Cultural values may prevent people from seeking psychotherapy if they do not accept the idea that talking about problems can relieve distress. Therapists have all heard prospective patients ask, "but how can just *talking* help?" If we were only talking about talking, the question would not be far off base. To benefit from therapy, patients have to talk *effectively* about their problems and how to solve them. Not everyone has these skills. Talking therapy is most useful for people who already know how to talk.

Life course and psychotherapy

As a consultant over the last 40 years, I have evaluated thousands of adults seeking psychotherapy. People may mark their progress in life according to an implicit set of expectations related to stages of adult development (Vaillant, 1977, 2002). My experience, paralleling that of other observers (Westen, 1998), is that therapy seekers are people who have had some degree of success in life, but who have failed to achieve stable intimacy. Thus, the typical therapy client tends to be a young or middle-aged person having difficulty finding a life partner, or sustaining an intimate relationship.

I worked for 25 years in a psychiatric service for university students that specialized in short-term psychotherapy. A large number of my patients were young people who sought help for what used to be called (and might still be called) a broken heart. Of course, that was not their only problem. But we live in an age where young people "try out" intimate relationships and postpone long-term commitments. That strategy, however wise in the long run, may not satisfy emotional needs in the short run. A young person can arrive at adulthood without ever having been able to have an intimate or meaningful relationship. People who have never been in love may begin to wonder if something is wrong. When one has been in love, but love has failed (perhaps more than once), one can feel pessimistic about the future.

I also cannot count the number of patients who have sought therapy around the time they reach the age of 30. Most have not been able to settle down in an intimate relationship. If a life task of this magnitude has not been mastered—particularly when the patient is a woman and the biological clock is ticking—talking therapy becomes more of an option.

Another common scenario is when people enter treatment while going through a divorce. Losing a spouse is a major stressor that may be disruptive for years—and not everyone ever gets over it. Yet while most of these patients are women, marital separation is more stressful for men, who become more isolated (Kalmijn, 2007).

The life events that bring people into therapy need not be unusual, but therapists can put them in a new context. They spend time sorting out personality traits, cognitive schema, and previous experiences to explain why people are more vulnerable to life stressors. But only those who already share a belief that talking is a way to handle distress will commit themselves to the process.

Two-thirds of psychotherapy patients are female. One reason may derive from consistent personality differences between the sexes (Larsen and Buss, 2008). Research on traits in different cultures (Costa et al., 2001) shows that women score higher on standard dimensions of neuroticism, agreeableness, warmth, and openness to feelings. In contrast, men are higher in assertiveness and openness to experience. By and large, women are better than men in talking about their feelings (Tannen, 1990), and more likely to prioritize interpersonal relationships (Cross and Madison, 1997). Men, who are more likely to seek status, can be reluctant to talk about feelings—partly out of lack of skill and partly out of fear of loss of face in the eyes of others (Baumeister and Sommer, 1997). In contrast, women seek talking therapy because even in an age of feminism, intimacy remains an imperative, and the biological clock provides a narrow window for procreation. Many yearn for love, and some live by it. Others do not want to grow old without bearing a child.

Long-term therapy

Short-term therapy has a plan, a purpose, and an endpoint. Patients receiving a brief course of treatment can use it to achieve a specific goal. Its evidence-base is strong. In contrast, long-term therapy is an open-ended procedure that lacks scientific support. It is this form of treatment that has given talking therapy a bad name.

Even after the decline of psychoanalysis, some patients seek treatment with no time limit. Unfortunately, Olfson et al.'s (2002) survey did not analyze their data separately for long-term psychotherapy (which they defined as more than 20 sessions). Thus, we have no empirical data to describe differences between those who seek lengthier treatment and those who use therapy to manage a crisis. My clinical impression is that the search for long-term therapy occurs when emotional needs are not being met in the outside world, and when psychotherapy is seen as a safer place to find it.

The American psychologist William Schofield (1964), who wrote a book provocatively entitled *Psychotherapy: The Purchase of Friendship*, suggested that therapists offer people a relationship that has become increasingly difficult to find. In real life, nobody is willing to listen to your problems for 45 minutes. Your friends and relatives will not tolerate hearing complaints for long before changing the subject. One psychoanalyst's arch comment on the idea that therapy might be a form of friendship was: "But where would you find such a friend?"

The most often quoted concept in Schofield's book was his proposal that people who seek psychotherapy tend to be "YAVIS"—that is, young, attractive, verbal, intelligent, and successful. While it is possible that this profile has been changing in recent decades, the survey data quoted above still support it. People who are verbal and intelligent are more likely to be interested in therapy. If they are successful, they will be able to afford it. Being attractive is also part of success. And by and large seekers of long-term therapy are not losers. Instead, they are winners who are not satisfied with their winnings.

The long and short of therapy

The problem with open-ended psychotherapy is that once it starts, it is difficult to know when to stop. In his early days, Freud treated patients fairly briefly. As late as the 1930s, two American psychiatrists (Kardiner, 1977; Wortis, 1984) who wrote books about their own analyses with Freud described treatment lasting about six months. But since not all patients got better in that time frame, Freud gradually lengthened psychoanalysis. The problem was that therapy began to stretch on indefinitely. In the end, longer was not necessarily better. In a paper written toward the end of his life, Freud (1937/1962) wondered whether there was something "interminable" about the method.

Every therapist since has faced the same question. Talking therapy does not usually cure. If it nonetheless provides relief, some people might "quit while they are ahead". Woody Allen's cinematic satires of psychotherapy going on for years without end described an all-too-common reality. For some people psychotherapy is not just a tool, but a way of life. As the witticism goes, "life is the disease and analysis is the cure".

Research on psychotherapy supports a time frame that does not exceed six months (Mackenzie, 1996). Good results usually take effect rapidly, and most goals can be met within a reasonable period of time.

The question is what to do for patients who do *not* get better in six months. Should they go to another therapist and try a different approach? Would they recover if given more time? Or is there a law of diminishing returns, so that people who don't improve in a few months fail to recover, even if they come for years?

My teachers encouraged me to continue treatment until patients were "ready" to leave. Of course, most people do leave when they feel better. But others hang on, hoping for more. There is an intrinsic tendency for the treatment to keep going. There are always new problems to talk about. (Life never really gives us a break.) And while old problems may be partially resolved, they can reoccur.

Long-term therapy without a time limit is no longer supported by insurance. At one time, federal government employees in Washington, DC were partially (or almost entirely) covered for an unlimited number of therapy sessions—and some used that privilege to go into taxpayer-supported psychoanalysis (Halpert, 1972). Over time these benefits were withdrawn. Today, most people in the United States who have managed care plans are covered for at least six, but for not more than 20 sessions a year. And in Canada, while there are no restrictions on length, a limited number of insured providers ensures that long-term therapy remains a rare procedure.

An expensive and time-consuming procedure like open-ended therapy can only be accessible to a few. In that respect it resembles other "heroic" treatments, such as cardiac surgery. Traditional psychoanalysis, on the average, takes five–six years (Doidge et al., 2002). At three sessions weekly, the total cost could come to $200,000, or more. That is why its market niche remains small, and why few practitioners exclusively devote their time to it.

A generation ago, Janet Malcolm (1982) wrote a book entitled *The Impossible Profession,* which described how experienced psychoanalysts in New York City could no longer fill their practices. Psychoanalytically oriented psychotherapy once or twice a week is much cheaper, and the *Consumer Reports* survey (Seligman, 1995) showed that many appreciate this form of treatment. But even at a lower frequency, most people cannot afford this kind of therapy.

The bottom line is that there is no strong scientific evidence supporting the effectiveness of treatment lasting for more than a year. To be fair, hardly any one has taken the trouble and expense to carry out research that could answer this question. The ideal way to test the effectiveness of longer therapy would be to assign patients randomly to therapies of different durations, and that has only been done in small-scale studies, with equivocal results (Knekt et al., 2008).

A meta-analysis by Leichsenring and Rabung, 2008), combining the findings of several clinical trials, as well as some observational studies, was published in a noted medical journal (Journal of the American Medical Association (JAMA)), and garnered a fair amount of attention. The authors concluded that therapy lasting for at least one year is specifically effective for what the authors called "complex disorders", that is, chronic conditions such as personality disorders and eating disorders.

Some psychoanalysts responded to this article by saying, "you see, we were right all along". But the report was flawed, and its conclusions were challenged in several letters to JAMA. The meta-analysis combined results from 23 small-sample studies representing many different diagnoses and many different treatments. Also, it did not require that analyses be conducted on the basis of "intention-to-treat"—a method used in clinical trials to ensure that patients who drop out of therapy are counted. Finally, the analysis did not systematically compare the effects of longer treatments to brief therapy.

I have little doubt that *some* patients do better in a year or so than in six months, and do not rule out extending psychotherapy for patients under certain conditions. In spite of my doubts, I continue to do so for a few patients. But brief therapy should be the default condition, and there is little or no scientific basis for prescribing *in advance* psychotherapy that will last several years. Moreover, long-term therapy should be reviewed regularly, probably with formal re-examination and independent review every six months.

To understand why therapy can be interminable, consider that some people who seek treatment are lonely and that others desire perfection. But in real life, we may have to find alternatives to intimacy, and some dreams never come true—a child who was never born, or a promotion that was never offered. The therapist's job is not to make everything possible but to help people live within their limitations.

It is easier to leave therapy when you have a life, which usually involves a job and connection to a community. For those who have found an intimate relationship, it is easier to terminate. You may never confide in someone else in quite the same way as you did to a therapist—but then you may not need to.

Part II
Modernity

5
Modernity and Psychotherapy

The birth of psychotherapy occurred at a time when the world became modern—or, more precisely, when the pace of modernization accelerated. What do we mean by modernity? This term has been variously defined, but generally refers to cultural changes associated with industrial and post-industrial society, by a decline in the influence of tradition and social norms. The sociologist Anthony Giddens (1998, p. 27) defines it as "a shorthand term for modern society, or industrial civilization" going on to state that "it is associated with (1) a certain set of attitudes towards the world, the idea of the world as open to transformation, by human intervention; (2) a complex of economic institutions, especially industrial production and a market economy; (3) a certain range of political institutions, including the nation-state and mass democracy."

Modernity has been a subject of intensive study by social scientists (Lilla, 2007) and by philosophers (Taylor, 1989, 1991, 2007). The changes associated with modernity have profoundly affected human psychology. The modern world is vastly more dynamic than any previous type of social order. Giddens (1998, p. 27) described a society that "unlike any preceding culture, lives in the future, rather than the past". To put it another way, people identify less with collective values and replace them with individual choices. Individualism, the key aspect of modernity, is a point of view that has shaped the development of psychotherapy.

While modernity is a complex phenomenon, the decline of organized religion is of particular relevance for talking therapy. Nearly a century ago, the German sociologist Max Weber stated: "The fate of our times is characterized by rationalization and intellectualization and, above all, by the disenchantment of the world" (Weber, 1918). Thus as religion became less influential, it left an empty niche. Talking therapy came to take over some of its healing functions, becoming a secular faith offering redemption through self-understanding.

How modernity developed

The world is always changing. Differences between modern and traditional societies are relative, not absolute. But while the conditions of life have not necessarily been stable in any period of history, the modern world is different because it espouses different values.

Most scholars trace the origins of modernity back to the Renaissance, but its key ideas were developed in the 18th-century Enlightenment (Johnson, 1990). Most historical and sociological literature has focused on the rapidly accelerating changes that marked the 19th and 20th centuries and are associated with the rise of industry and capitalism. While these observations concern Europe and North America, the social change associated with modernity has now become global.

The modern world has produced unprecedented social and economic progress. We are very fortunate to live in such a society. But for some people, modernity has a dark side. Life may have been more uncertain in the past, but there was greater certainty about values. Nothing can be taken for granted, and everything is subject to modification. Those who can cope with change will thrive on modernity. Others may lose their moorings.

The Irish poet, William Butler Yeats, described this aspect of modernity in his famous poem, *The Second Coming*:

> Things fall apart; the centre cannot hold;
> Mere anarchy is loosed upon the world,
> The blood-dimmed tide is loosed, and everywhere
> The ceremony of innocence is drowned;
> The best lack all conviction, while the worst
> Are full of passionate intensity.

The decline of organized religion may be the most important consequence of modernity. On an emotional level, it can be difficult to compensate for a loss of belief. Yet people have had to learn to do without faith, at the cost of a hole in the psyche. These trends were already apparent in the 19th century, but are only one aspect of a wider loss of meaning and social belonging. Karl Marx described a lack of connection between the self and the world he called "alienation" (Meszaros,

1992). The French sociologist Emile Durkheim (1897/1997) described a decrease in social norms he termed "anomie". In the early 20th century, the German sociologist Ferdinand Tonnies (2001) described the replacement of social associations in which individuals are oriented to a group to one shaped by self-interest, as a shift from "*gemeinschaft*" to "*gesellschaft*". All these observers were "on to something" about the darker side of modernity.

The United States has been the most modern of all societies. It was created by a sharp break with the past, and its subsequent history was shaped by migration and immigration (Schamma, 2008; Wright, 2008). As early as the 1830s, the French historian Alexis de Tocqueville (1837/2000) toured the country and described a striking egalitarianism and individual freedom that distinguished it from Europe.

Individualism is the most striking aspect of American culture. However, Fischer (2010) suggests this characteristic might better be called "voluntarism". Thus while Americans still become attached to groups and networks, they do so voluntarily, not, as in many traditional societies, because they are required to. If modernity and individualism reached an apogee in the United States, it is no accident that psychotherapy had its greatest influence there. What could be more individualistic than spending many hours talking about one's inner world in the hope of self-improvement? Only in recent decades, as European societies have become less traditional, psychotherapy has found a more prominent place there (Zerbetto and Tantam, 2001). And as modernity spreads to developing countries, we can expect to see a growth of psychotherapy across the globe. There is indeed evidence that this is happening (Wedding, 2007), given that therapists find clients in large cities all over the world.

As modernity became global, many parts of the world have come to resemble the West. But the process remains incomplete. Many recent immigrants to North America and Europe come from parts of the world only recently touched by modern values. Therapists see some of them as patients in their practices. Most will be less individualistic than North Americans or Europeans, more oriented toward family and community, and less likely to seek psychotherapy. And their children may be only partially acculturated.

Understanding culture sheds light on why talking therapy is such a modern phenomenon. Until recently, in most non-Western societies, life did not change dramatically from one generation to the next. Social scientists have distinguished *traditional* societies, with high social cohesion, fixed social roles, and intergenerational continuity, from *modern* societies, with lower social cohesion, fluid social roles, and less continuity between generations. While this is a very broad distinction, it has been generally supported by large-scale surveys, such as the World Values Study (Ingelhardt and Abramson, 1995). Needless to say, traditional societies differ from each other and are far from immune to internal tensions. Nevertheless, they deviate from modern societies in having stronger shared social values and norms.

In the course of history, most societies have been "traditional" in one way or another. But with the march of globalization, few remained so. While developing societies have also influenced Western culture, they have come to take on many of the characteristics of the developed world. One might say that the entire world is in the process of embracing modernity (Berman, 1982; Southall, 1998). And what we are seeing is not just change itself, but an *increasing rate* of change (Haferkamp and Smelser, 1992).

Traditional societies, while they can be as different from each other as from modern societies, have important common features. In a traditional society, people did not have to "find themselves" or define a unique identity. Life choices were shaped by family members and by the wisdom of elders. People living in such societies would have had a niche defined from them. They would not have needed to look, or think of looking, for psychotherapy.

It would be a mistake to idealize traditional societies as more harmonious than our own. That has been a kind of cottage industry for urbanites who believe in a rural paradise spoiled by civilization, or believe that indigenous populations had wisdom that has been lost and were somehow "in harmony with nature". The reality is that every culture has had its own problems. The belief that violence is a modern problem is particularly untrue. Murder rates in most parts of the world were much higher in the past than they are today (Monkkonen, 2001; Pinker, 2011). People with severe mental illnesses were usually mistreated (Shorter, 1997), while psychological problems were often dismissed. One might quote James Joyce's epigram: "history is a nightmare from which we have just begun to awake."

Life in traditional societies could also be unhappy, albeit in a different way. Societies with rigid hierarchies benefited those who fit in or had the skills to find a useful social niche. But people who did not fit in could end up isolated. In fact, most modern people would not be comfortable in a traditional society. The rich and powerful had control over personal choices, there was no escape from oppression, and most would probably die young. Many parts of the world are like that—even today. The main upside was that everyone had a place—even if it was a poor one.

When I was young, I had an opportunity to live for almost two years in a fairly traditional society. I joined the American Peace Corps and was assigned to the state of Kerala, in the southern part of India. This was a very different world. Although Kerala has the highest educational level in India, and women have attained most of the same rights as men, the influence of caste remains very strong, and the social fabric has not been modernized to the same extent as in cities like Mumbai or Delhi. In some ways, Kerala society in the 1960s resembled the West 200 years ago. While most people's lives were constrained by caste and power, these structures provided them with a sense of belonging. There was little need in such a society for talking therapy; even today hardly any psychotherapists practice there.

Modern society is good for those who know how to take advantage of it—but not so good for those who lack that ability. Contemporary people are geographically mobile, often live far from extended families, and have more tenuous attachments to community (Walmsley, 1988). Elders and traditions no longer function as guides, and it is more difficult to find meaning in devotion to a faith or service to a community. Moreover, when occupations and marital partners are a matter of personal choice, making decisions can be difficult—and they often turn out to be wrong. Is it then any wonder how many people seek psychotherapy?

Religion and psychotherapy

In any society, people find meaning through connection and community. Traditionally, the primary base of that community was organized religion. Today, in most Western countries, and particularly in Europe, formal adherence to faith has greatly fallen (Ingelhardt and Abramson, 1995). The United States is a prominent exception (Norris and Inglehart, 2004). Although founded by non-practicing Protestants (such as George Washington) and Deists (such as Thomas Jefferson), American culture later became influenced by Christian revivalism. Even so, these trends can be understood as *responses* to the challenges of modernity, in a society that had moved far away from tradition.

Organized religion is a creative force that has produced some of the greatest cultural achievements of Western civilization. Many people continue to believe and retain strong links with churches. Moreover, there is a strong correlation between religious affiliation and better mental health (Koenig, 2001). This relationship could reflect the effects of faith, of a sense of belonging, or both.

Today, about 60% of people living in the United States report that religious belief plays a major role in their life (Pew Global Attitudes Project, 2007). Nonetheless, the fact that 40% do *not* consider religion important is notable. (That would *not* have been true in the past.) And an increasing number of people in the United States describe themselves as "spiritual" rather than belonging to any specific sect (Hout and Fischer, 2002). The most recent American Religious identification Survey (2009) showed a similar decline, with 15% declaring no religion at all, while 27% do not even plan for a religious funeral.

The current influence of organized religion in the modern world cannot be compared to the past, when priests and ministers could exert some degree of control over many aspects of private and public life. Religion has become a matter of private belief, not a guiding force in public behavior. At the same time, the continued interest in Eastern religions and philosophy underlines the weakness of Western traditions. Also, it is not clear whether religious evangelism in the United States is a stable trend or a defensive stance that will not stand the test of time.

The power of belief in the modern world declined most strikingly among intellectuals, a trend already apparent in the 19th century. The Victorian poet Matthew Arnold described it beautifully in his poem *Dover Beach* (which is famous because it describes modernity so well):

> The Sea of Faith
> Was once, too, at the full, and round earth's shore
> Lay like the folds of a bright girdle furled.
> But now I only hear
> Its melancholy, long, withdrawing roar,
> Retreating, to the breath
> Of the night-wind, down the vast edges drear
> And naked shingles of the world.

Arnold thought that the solution to the loss of faith lay in intimacy:

> Ah, love, let us be true
> To one another! For the world, which seems
> To lie before us like a land of dreams,
> So various, so beautiful, so new,
> Hath really neither joy, nor love, nor light,
> Nor certitude, nor peace, nor help for pain;

And we are here as on a darkling plain
Swept with confused alarms of struggle and flight,
Where ignorant armies clash by night.

But Arnold was wrong to think that the problems of modernity could be solved by romantic attachment. As will be discussed later in this book, relying on one person for all your emotional needs is problematic. People who believe (with the Beatles) that "all you need is love" may actually be more likely to have failed relationships.

If love is not "the answer", psychotherapy becomes even more important. The rituals of talking to a therapist can at least partially fill the niche left empty by the absence of connection. Therapy appeals to people who are searching for meaning and offers a powerful *weltanschauung* of its own.

Psychotherapy is not the only secular religion in the modern world—Marxism has been another claimant, and it also offered a chance to sacrifice oneself for a higher cause (Furet, 1999). In both cases, believers could consult sacred texts, deify founders, and believe in the transformation of human nature. The difference from traditional religion was that Marxist redemption would take place on earth, not in Heaven.

For most of its practitioners, psychotherapy has had more modest goals. Freud (1896/1957) famously stated that his treatment only aimed "to turn neurotic misery into normal human unhappiness". Freud was a pessimist about the human condition. But that did not stop his followers, as well as those who developed other schools of treatment, from claiming that psychotherapy has the potential to make happiness universal. In this way, the movement came to have a vision of universal redemption.

This was a striking feature of the psychoanalytic movement, which created an elect priesthood to guard a sacred vision. Some parts of the movement were clearly redemptive. The British psychoanalyst Melanie Klein thought that if every child was analyzed at an early age, mental illness could be completely prevented (Grosskurth, 1984).

The need for passionate belief cannot easily be suppressed. Even if psychoanalysis claimed to be scientific, it was much more like a religion. And almost every school of therapy since Freud has risen on its own wave of faith. The field fragmented into hundreds of methods, some of which evolved into cults. Like competing churches, each claimed to have found the truth. And beginning with Freud, there was a tendency to see anyone who disagreed with these new ideas as either ignorant or resistant to the truth. Too many psychotherapists have suffered from unjustified certainty about their beliefs.

How therapy replaced religion

Phillip Rieff, an influential American social critic in the 1960s, was one of the first intellectuals to note that psychotherapy had replaced religion as a guide to living in Western culture. In his book *The Triumph of the Therapeutic*, Rieff (1966) described the rise of a "psychological man" who does not adhere to traditional culture. He observed that before the 20th century, most people thought that even if existence is full of suffering, life fits into a divine plan. But with the "death of God", everyone had to create their own meaning. With little to go on, some sought professional guidance—in much the same way as their ancestors sought the comfort of belief and tradition.

Individualism began as an urban phenomenon, and for a long time rural areas remained more traditional. But now modernity seems to affect almost every corner of the Western world, not to speak of the globe, "Americanizing" the entire world. I have seen some of these changes in my own lifetime, and they seem to follow the decline of religion.

Although I grew up in the United States, I have lived most of my life in the Canadian province of Québec, which used to be a highly traditional and religious society. When I first arrived there to go to medical school in the 1960s, one could hardly see a movie in full, since Catholic priests heavily censored every film. Then, in the course of the 1960s, a "Quiet Revolution" led to a complete repudiation of religious traditions, followed by a rapid shift in values (Gauvreau, 2007). Church attendance is now very low, and Québec has become the most "modern" part of Canada. Roman Catholicism may have been around for two millennia, but its recent decline in developed countries has been dramatic. Most people in Québec live in a totally secular world. The largest number of psychoanalysts in the country live there, and there is no part of Canada with a stronger interest in psychotherapy of all kinds.

Modernity, personality, and symptoms

Modernity does not affect everyone in the same way, but it produces winners and losers. In this way it functions as a kind of *selection pressure*. Most people cope with change, but a vulnerable sub-population is at risk. For example, Klerman and Weissman (1989) documented a striking increase in rates of depression in the community after the Second World War. These changes are almost certainly due to social stressors. Ehrenberg (2010) has suggested that cultural expectations created by modernity have made depression more prevalent.

However, not everyone reacts in the same way to circumstance. The ability of people to adapt to change depends on their personality. Psychologists have long studied how people differ on personality traits. Using behavioral genetic methods, they have found that about half of the variance in these traits is genetic in origin, while the other half depends on the environment (Plomin et al., 2001). Thus even if the twig is bent, the social environment determines the final shape of the tree.

The most basic personality traits are extraversion (how much one requires contact with other people), neuroticism (how easily one gets upset), as well as conscientiousness and agreeableness (Costa and Widiger, 2001). These traits can work either for or against you, depending on social context. But introverted and neurotic traits are problematic in modern society because they make it more difficult to adapt to change. These characteristics, as well as low agreeableness and conscientiousness, are associated with most forms of psychopathology (Costa and Widiger, 2001). People with these traits are more sensitive to adversity, and less likely to develop support networks. Yet many of them would have functioned perfectly well in traditional societies. But the modern world does not consistently provide back-up systems. It favors those with an extraverted and optimistic bent. These characteristics have never been at such a premium.

Temperament and personality limit the range of symptoms that can develop in an individual. As discussed in earlier chapters, one can distinguish between internalizing problems (distress experienced within the self) and externalizing problems (distress acted out in relation to other people). The social environment plays an important role in shaping these patterns: in Western society, externalizing symptoms are becoming more prominent over time. A large body of data shows that people in traditional societies tend to develop more internalizing symptoms under stress, while people in modern societies are more likely to show externalizing symptoms (Tsai et al., 2001). Thus, the more you are attached to your social community, the more you will suffer internally. In contrast, the more individualistic you are, the more you will "act out" your problems.

Severe mental illnesses such as schizophrenia, melancholia, and bipolar disorder do not show so much variability, and these conditions are found in all societies (Murphy, 1982). But some diagnoses can be "culture-bound", that is, seen only in some societies and not in others (Prince and Tseng-Laroche, 1990). Most illnesses lie between these two extremes. The basic forms are universal, but their prevalence changes with time and circumstance. Mental disorders with that pattern can be described as being "socially sensitive", while disorders with a more stable prevalence across culture and time can be described as being "socially insensitive" (Paris, 2004).

Some of the most socially sensitive disorders are substance abuse, mood disorders, eating disorders, and impulsive personality disorders. Changes in prevalence of these conditions over relatively brief periods of time (single generations) clearly demonstrate the role of social change (Paris, 1996a). And all are characterized by externalizing symptoms. These disorders are contained by social structures and amplified by their absence, making them particularly responsive to social context. Disorders characterized by internalizing symptoms (unipolar depression; anxiety disorders) are somewhat more universal, but can also be responsive to social context. And some diagnoses, such as post-traumatic stress disorder, are social constructions that allow people to express distress in specific and culturally sanctioned ways (Young, 1995).

A second (and stronger) line of evidence for the effects of social factors on mental disorders comes from cross-cultural research. For example, antisocial personality disorder is much less prevalent in relatively traditional societies such as Taiwan (Compton et al., 1991) or Japan (Sato and Takeichi, 1993) than in North America or Western Europe. But needless to say, the links between risk factors and symptoms are not simple, since so many other factors come into play. These relationships are as complex as history itself.

Nonetheless, the effects of rapid social change on psychological symptoms have been documented by epidemiological research. After 1945, rates of crime, substance abuse, and depression in most Western countries increased among the young in both the United States and Europe (Millon, 1993; Rutter and Smith, 1995). These changes were paralleled by increases, beginning about 1960, in the prevalence of attempted and completed suicide (Bland et al., 1998).

Increases in psychological symptoms over a short period of time *must* reflect changes in the social fabric. Something happened in the postwar years that made it more difficult to be young. Since these changes occurred during a period of unprecedented prosperity, one can eliminate an economic explanation. These developments are more likely to be attributable to rapid social change, particularly the disruption of family and social networks (Rutter and Smith, 1995). Notably, this was also a time when psychotherapy became more influential.

Needless to say, life did not only become stressful in 1945. In the 19th century, George Miller Beard had explained the prevalence of neurasthenia (or what we would now call chronic fatigue syndrome) as the result of railroads and other new technologies that made life frenetic and exhausting too (Schuster, 2003). But the pace of social change greatly accelerated over the next century or so.

In summary, there have always been—and will always be—mental illnesses, but social forces can increase their prevalence. In a classic study, Leighton et al. (1963) found that communities that suffered from "social disintegration" (i.e., the breakdown of structures that provide identity and connection) had higher rates of psychological symptoms than those where these structures remained intact.

By and large, there is no reason to believe that modern life produces an *overall* higher level of psychopathology than a traditional society. Life is neither happier nor unhappier, but different. Rather, social forces may determine the *form* that symptoms take, as well as the *threshold* at which specific disorders develop (Murphy, 1982; Shorter, 1997).

The form that psychological symptoms take varies over time. Shorter (1997) proposed that each historical and cultural period has a "symptom pool" through which patients express distress, based on whatever is current in the social milieu. Some symptoms are shaped by a mechanism of "social contagion" (Levy and Nail, 1993). Two good examples are bulimia and wrist-cutting, behavioral patterns that patients can learn about through magazines, cinema, and television.

To the surprise of many experts, the prevalence of crime, substance abuse, and suicide have been going *down* in the last 20 years (Zimring, 2006; Kutcher and Szumilas, 2008). Even child abuse, a sensitive marker for social disruption, is becoming less common (Finkelhor and Jones, 2006). How can we explain these salutary changes? Perhaps, as we accommodate to new social conditions, the impact of modernity has reached a plateau. If so, the need for psychotherapy could also undergo change.

Youth, modernity, and psychotherapy

By and large, the young bear the brunt of modernity. Most psychotherapy patients are young adults (Henry et al., 1971). Ironically, while modern culture idealizes youth, young people tend to be more unhappy than their elders. Large-scale epidemiological studies in the United

States show that the most common psychological symptoms in adults peak between ages 20 and 40 and then decrease (Kessler et al., 2005a). This pattern may be partly neurodevelopmental, but could also reflect some of the strains of modernity, in which intergenerational discontinuities require young people to establish occupational and social roles without easy access to community support.

Over 100 years ago G. Stanley Hall (1904) introduced the concept of adolescence as a distinct developmental stage. It was only at that point that the lack of continuity between the generations in the modern world became notable. Once a simple transition from childhood to adulthood, the adolescent years began to be seen as associated with rebellion, alienation, and a search for identity.

Actually few teenagers suffer from a turbulent life. Research in school populations has found (to the surprise of many) that most adolescents love their parents and have little interest in rebellion (Offer and Offer, 1975; Furstenberg, 2000). Even so, the minority who experience symptoms may not do well in the long run—in the most vulnerable individuals, psychological problems rarely disappear in adulthood (Cohen et al., 2005). Many mental disorders begin in adolescence. But the teenage years are not usually a time to seek psychotherapy. That option usually comes later, when young adults attain a sufficient level of independence to be comfortable with the idea of needing help.

Why is it more difficult to be young today than 100 years ago? Throughout most of history, young people assumed adult roles shortly after puberty. In traditional societies, adolescents and young adults usually did the same work as their parents. Thus, the young were *provided* with social roles. They lived in extended families, villages, and tribes and rarely traveled far. Moreover, young people did not have to search very far to find intimate relationships. Marriage was arranged and occurred early in life, and partners were chosen from the same or neighboring communities.

In contrast, young people in modern societies spend many years learning how to function as adults. They are not provided with an identity or a social role and rarely do the same work as their parents. They have to learn necessary skills from strangers. Families may not understand the nature of their children's careers. And young people have to find their own mates, and since there is no guarantee that the search will be successful, many end up dealing with the vicissitudes of mistaken choices, hurtful rejections, and painful loneliness. Moreover, traditional choices of a mate through family connections, churches, or social networks are weaker today, sometimes replaced by on-line dating and social media. We may be amused at matrimonial advertisements in non-Western societies, but they can lead to more stable relationships than free choice. To some extent, marital stability reflected sanctions against divorce. But as we will see, marriage is best protected when nested in a context of extended family and community.

Most of us would be unhappy in a society that did not allow us to choose an occupation and a life partner. But those who are temperamentally vulnerable pay a price for freedom. It is difficult for impulsive people to choose a career, for moody people to deal with the cruelty and rejection of peers, and for shy people to find intimate relationships. If you cannot accomplish these tasks on your own, no one will do them for you.

Another challenging aspect of the modern world is the way it confronts individuals with a disorienting set of options (Gergen, 1991). Liberty of choice is exciting for some and frightening for others. One can never be sure that one has made a correct choice. Modern young people may agonize as to whether they have chosen the "right" career or the "right" lover. As psychotherapists know, some patients delay choices (or fail to follow through on their commitments) for this very reason. Patients may also seek treatment to address these difficulties.

While choice is usually a plus, some prefer to "escape from freedom" (Fromm, 1941), that is, to submerge their identity in great causes, such as radical political movements, or the religious absolutisms that have arisen to challenge secular Western society. Zealotry is as much about identity as belief. If you have absolute faith in the literal truth of a book or dogma, you never need to feel alienated.

Faced with a confusing world where families and communities cannot guide them, some develop symptoms, and some seek help through psychotherapy. Some young people feel overwhelmed and confused by the demands of the modern world. They may seek guidance from an older (and hopefully wiser) psychotherapist.

In summary, modernity is probably more stressful for those who seek psychotherapy. The patients that therapists see are much less likely to be formally religious (Frank and Frank, 1991). In the past, meaning came through community, and people lived under the "great tent" of tradition. As this protection became tattered, psychotherapy was called on to fill this niche. Most patients come for help with problems with intimacy. But while the need for intense romantic love, with all the expectations that this creates, have taken on an unprecedented level of importance in the modern world, relationships are more difficult to sustain. This problem can only be partially managed by psychotherapy.

In a classic study of trends in modern society, the American sociologist Robert Putnam (2000) described an increasing deficit in "social capital", that is, connections within (and between) social networks. Putnam emphasized the particular vulnerability of people who lack social skills. If networks are not built into society, not everyone can develop them on their own. The title of Putnam's book, *Bowling Alone*, is a metaphor that also describes a reality (Americans still bowl, but are less likely to join bowling teams). Research has confirmed the principle that social capital is associated with mental health (De Silva et al., 2005).

In summary, most people in modern society can no longer depend on guidance from priests, family elders, or community leaders. Although only a minority of the population ever seeks psychotherapy, hundreds of thousands have done so. The paradox is that modernity creates needs that psychotherapy can never entirely fulfill.

6
Narcissism: Individual and Cultural

Defining narcissism

Sigmund Freud (1914/1959) used the term "narcissism" to describe a universal psychological mechanism of self-love and self-absorption. But narcissism is also a trait, a personality characteristic that varies from one person to another and that can work either for people or against them.

A certain degree of narcissism can be helpful in life, and some people have too little. Like any trait, it belongs to a range of behavioral patterns that have been naturally selected and that can be adaptive or maladaptive under different conditions (Beck and Freeman, 2002). Thus, to be impulsive or cautious, extraverted or introverted, can be either helpful or unhelpful depending on context and circumstance. Healthy narcissism is associated with ambition and assertiveness. Unhealthy narcissism is associated with grandiosity and insensitivity. Thus narcissism is good in moderation, but bad in excess. A reasonable dose is associated with healthy functioning. A large dose leads to trouble.

Narcissists have many problems, but may not be aware of them. When challenged about behaviors, they are more likely to be angry than sorry. They may not feel particularly guilty about selfish conduct, or even view themselves as selfish. They simply fail to understand why other people do not see things the same way.

Yet narcissists can be impressive—at least in the short run. Research shows that they are initially attractive to others (Back et al., 2010). But in the long run, excessive self-regard turns other people off. Most of us are self-involved when young, but learn from experience how to be better people, particularly when we form attachments to a community (Finkel et al., 2009). In contrast, narcissists refuse to mature. Some come to therapy not to change their personality but to reinforce it. Their self-absorption can have tragic consequences. The narcissist becomes trapped in a mirror of self and finds no way to escape.

Research on narcissism

While many therapists have written books about narcissism, most are based on clinical impressions, not data. Only a few researchers (e.g., Gunderson et al., 1995; Russ et al., 2008; Cain et al., 2008; Twenge and Campbell, 2009) have studied this trait with reliable measurement tools.

Personality as a whole is a profile of traits that distinguish one individual from another—affecting emotion, behavior, and thought in a variety of contexts and shaping the way that psychological distress is experienced. One research method for studying personality is behavior genetics, which determines the extent to which identical twins are more similar than fraternal twins, creating an estimate of heritability (Plomin et al., 2001). About half of the variability in most traits is heritable (Costa and Widiger, 2001). That is one reason why two children growing up in the same family have different personality profiles (Dunn and Plomin, 1993). The other half of the variability in personality traits derives from environmental factors, and most of that contribution is *unshared*, that is, unique to the individual's history, while a much smaller part is *shared* within the same family. These principles have been shown to apply to narcissistic traits (Cain et al., 2008).

No one is born to be narcissistic. But children with certain temperamental characteristics may be more vulnerable. To avoid that outcome, children and young people need strong families and strong social structures. In this way, pathological narcissism emerges from interactions between temperament, life experience, and social forces.

The origins of narcissism

The psychoanalyst Otto Kernberg may not be a scientist, but he has had thoughtful things to say about narcissism. One is that you cannot be narcissistic unless you have something to be narcissistic *about* (Kernberg, 1976). You might be smart, good-looking, or have an unusual talent of some kind. If so, that might make it possible, from an early age, to over-invest your sense of worth in whatever about yourself is special.

It has long been thought that parenting practices can reinforce narcissism. In other words, children can be "spoiled". That idea has gone out of fashion, as much of what previous generations would have considered over-indulgent has become mainstream parenting. Modern therapy culture has made us afraid of displeasing our children (Furedi, 2008). And some researchers believe that modern parents are promoting narcissism by providing too much praise and too little criticism (Twenge, 2006).

In the 1970s, narcissism became a major subject for psychoanalysis. New ideas became influential, and in some ways remain so. Heinz Kohut (1970, 1977) thought that narcissism develops as a defensive stance against low self-esteem, due to parental emotional neglect, lack of empathy, and a failure to "mirror" emotions. Having a grandiose image of the self might be a way of saying, "no one can really hurt me, since I am so special and talented". Some parents may provide *conditional* mirroring, in that they are over-concerned with the success of their child (Miller, 1984). In that scenario, a grandiose self-image says "I can please my parents and everybody else by being special, even if that means ignoring other needs." Otto Kernberg took a darker view of narcissism. He explained it as a temperamental variant, reinforced by cold parents. But he also suggested that this trait develops when the individual has "some special talent that becomes a refuge against the basic feelings of being unloved" (Kernberg, 1976, p. 235). However, recent research has suggested that parental permissiveness is associated with the *grandiose* aspects of narcissism, while over-control is more associated with a second element, describing being thin-skinned and that has been called *vulnerable* narcissism (Horton et al., 2006; Horton, 2011).

Yet parenting cannot, by itself, explain why people become narcissistic. Studies of siblings (Dunn and Plomin, 1998) show that one child in a family can be self-centered, while another can be quiet, hard-working, and persistent. If parents play a role here, it lies in their reaction to differences in temperament between their children. Moreover, as any parent can attest, *all* children are self-centered—they are programmed to put their own needs first. But most people become less narcissistic with maturity. Only a few grow into adults who consider themselves special and entitled.

Crucially, narcissistic traits may not become problematic unless society at large supports them. The importance of social context is demonstrated by the way the trait can sometimes develop later in life. In a scenario sometimes termed "acquired situational narcissism", people who were humble prior to becoming wealthy or famous may develop narcissistic traits if they live in an environment that promotes them. Since I do not treat people who are rich and famous, I can't provide an example from my own practice. But one only has to read the papers to see how some people come to believe in their own publicity.

Narcissistic personality disorder

When personality traits seriously interfere with interpersonal dysfunction and work performance, one can diagnose a disorder. In the standard manual of psychiatric diagnosis *Diagnostic Manual for Mental Disorders, fourth edition, Text Revision* (DSM-IV-TR; American Psychiatric Association, 2000), personality disorders are defined as ways of thinking, feeling, and behaving that create dysfunction in work and relationships in many contexts over many years. Patients meeting criteria for the specific diagnosis of narcissistic personality disorder (NPD) are described as having a "pervasive pattern of grandiosity, need for admiration, and lack of empathy". Grandiosity is the central feature: needing to be the best and to have the best, to be entitled, and to have the right to put oneself first. Since narcissism is associated with a failure to make use of feedback when things go wrong, it interferes with the dialogue that makes psychotherapy work (Ogrodniczuk et al., 2009). The concept of NPD has inspired a small but respectable scientific literature (Wink et al., 2005; Cain et al., 2008, Ogrodniczuk et al., 2009; Campbell and Miller, 2011). The NPD diagnosis has aroused opposition, and at one point was at the point of being dropped in DSM-5, due to come out in 2013. However, NPD was restored to the manual in 2011, possibly because so many clinicians find it useful to describe patients who present this clinical picture.

The dysfunction in NPD comes from a lack of success in work and intimate relationships. If not admired, narcissists react by becoming angry, sulky, or contemptuous. They expect the world to share their self-admiration, and do not understand other's feelings, but focus on whether their own needs are being met. They are sorely lacking in empathy and perspective, which is why they often treat other people badly.

Even though narcissists tend to blame others for their troubles, they still seek psychotherapy. Beck and Freeman (2002) suggested that these patients come to treatment when depressed and defeated. And there are good reasons for narcissists to be prone to depression. Kernberg (1987) noted that they can be promising and attractive when young, but have trouble dealing with the inevitable disappointments and losses that come with aging. A narcissist who manages to remain successful may never seek or require professional help.

One might get the impression from observing politicians, celebrities, corporate executives, and business tycoons that inflated self-esteem can bring you to the top. But for every success, there are thousands of "wannabees" and "might-have-beens" who spend the rest of their life explaining why they could have been (and should have been) contenders. Thus most people with NPD, in spite of their ambition and self-promotion, do not do well in life (Cain et al., 2008).

In my work as a consultant, I have seen many people who achieved a degree of success while young, but were unable to sustain it. Some did well as employees, but failed when they tried to strike out on their own as entrepreneurs—grandiosity led them to take unrealistic risks. I have also seen many who faced losses in middle age and never worked again, unable to sustain blows to their pride or lower their expectations.

Since narcissists can be initially attractive, I have learned to be suspicious of my own reactions when anyone impresses me too quickly. Even so, narcissistic traits may have remained common in the population because they are adaptive. These individuals are more dominant, more charismatic, and more sexually attractive. But their intimate relationships tend to be unstable. There are no solid statistics about divorce rates in NPD, but my observation has been that these consequences go with the territory. Research shows that patients with NPD are distressed, lonely, and have poor social functioning (Miller et al., 2007). These are not the celebrities about whom we read in the media.

In the end, the Achilles heel of a narcissist lies in a failure of connection. Even among those who have achieved social status, moving from one relationship to another without permanence and commitment often leads to little but emptiness. While narcissism can get you started in life, it is not a trait that bodes well for the long run. People who need constant admiration can surround themselves with other people who support their grandiosity and ignore warnings about risks and consequences. But if you offer promise rather than performance, other people will be disappointed. Long-term success requires persistence and resilience. That is no less true in the modern age than it was in the past.

The treatment of NPD

Can NPD be successfully treated? The short answer is that we do not know. Patients who meet criteria for NPD comprise a minority in practice—about 5% of all patients, according to a survey in a large clinic (Zimmerman et al., 2008). And psychotherapy for this population has never been subjected to clinical trials.

Meanwhile psychoanalysts weighed in with their own ideas. Although these theories have never been empirically tested, they have had a significant influence on the way clinicians think. Kohut (1977) suggested that providing consistent empathy can modify narcissism. His theory of "self-psychology" was the basis for a method of psychotherapy, in which therapists always remain empathic, even when patients are difficult and contrary. The idea that understanding has curative power resembles the "client-centered therapy" developed by the American psychologist Carl Rogers (1951). Kernberg (1987) was more pessimistic (rightly so, in my opinion). His approach emphasizes confronting patients with the consequences of their world-view (a necessary but not necessarily successful intervention).

Narcissism declines with age (Foster et al., 2003), and most people learn to have more reasonable expectations of life as they mature. But the patients therapists see do *not* easily learn from experience. Some become more amenable to therapy after having lived long enough to learn that the world does not always go their way. Kernberg (1976) even described a sub-type that he called "malignant narcissism", which becomes worse, not better, over time.

None of the theories about NPD have led to effective treatment. The empirical literature (Ronningstam et al., 1998; Stone, 2006; Miller et al., 2007) supports the clinical impression that these patients are unusually difficult. They seek treatment when life goes badly for them, but do not readily engage in the self-criticism required to benefit from talking therapy.

Cultural narcissism and modernity

Narcissism is a problem for people as individuals. The larger issue is how this characteristic has come to pervade the attitudes and beliefs of *everyone*.

Christopher Lasch, a professor of history at the University of Rochester, introduced the term "cultural narcissism" (Lasch, 1979). He suggested that modern society encourages individuals to focus on self and to loosen ties to community, and noted that contemporary culture focuses on fame, celebrity, and riches (as opposed to duty, honor, and service). Synthesizing Marx and Freud, Lasch argued that social developments in the 20th century, associated with the growth of capitalism and the information revolution, amplify narcissistic personality traits. Modernity produces fragile self-concepts associated with a fear of commitment and lasting relationships, a dread of aging, and an excessive admiration for fame and celebrity. Like his predecessor Phillip Rieff (1966), Lasch was not a neutral scholar but a passionate social critic. His thesis was controversial, and he did not actually attempt to *prove* that modern society promotes narcissism. Nonetheless, the impact of his book shows that Lasch was on to something. While he has sometimes been dismissed as a curmudgeon uncomfortable with modernity, Lasch's ideas may be even more relevant now than in the 1970s.

Rieff (1966), who observed very similar trends, never used the term "narcissism". But he was the first observer of the development of a therapy culture linked to radical individualism, a concept later elaborated by Furedi (2004). Rieff noted that social virtue is less of an ideal in modern culture, while the well-being of the individuals has become paramount, and that a "therapeutic" orientation makes all truths contingent and negotiable, undermining shared social values. Writing decades before the rise of post-modernism, Rieff anticipated its attack on morality, science, and the very existence of truth (Gross and Levitt, 1994; Gross et al., 1997). When relativism is pushed to an extreme, the point of view of the individual is what counts, and personal preferences are more important than truth.

Ideas have a much broader impact when translated into the popular media. More people learned about the alienation of industrial labor from Charlie Chaplin's film *Modern Times* than from any book. Thus, the American critic and author Tom Wolfe (who is neither an academic nor a scholar) has presented the same thesis in a very popular format. In a widely quoted essay, Wolfe (1976) coined a term that has been used ever since to describe cultural narcissism—"The Me Decade". Wolfe's point was that a shift had occurred in the social fabric, in which people no longer bemoaned the loss of tradition, but actually came to *celebrate* narcissism. Wolfe thought that this increased focus on the self was the result of unprecedented post-war affluence.

The American psychologist Jean Twenge (2006; Twenge and Campbell, 2009) has been critical of the same social trends. Twenge expresses particular concern about concepts that emphasize raising self-esteem—without expectations of performance – and questions child-rearing practices in which parental praise is offered "unconditionally", a point previously made by Furedi (2004, 2008). Twenge also notes how media "therapists" such as "Dr. Phil", as well as influential personalities such as Oprah Winfrey, make pronouncements replete with "psychobabble" about the putative benefits of self-esteem but are contradicted by scientific research.

The common thread is that cultural narcissism makes the self more important than social commitments. Only a few intellectuals, for example, the Russian-American novelist Ayn Rand (1961), have considered selfishness to be a virtue. Even so, the idea that personal sacrifice is more important than self has fallen into decline.

Cultural narcissism is not entirely new. Establishing a balance between the needs of individuals and the expectations of society is a persistent theme in human history. In every epoch, ambitious people have indulged in self-display and sought fame (Baudry, 1986). But narcissists of the past were aristocrats with privilege and power. In the Roman Empire, Emperors and Senators could behave outrageously, but plebeians and slaves did not have that choice. Only in modern times could individuals lacking the advantage of birth rise rapidly to fame. The most famous example is Napoleon Bonaparte, an ambitious man who came out of nowhere to attain political power, but who could not give up seeking military glory, a need that eventually destroyed him. What may be unique about our own time is that narcissism is possible for *everyone* and that it may even gain a degree of social approval.

In this way, narcissism is a universal problem that has been exacerbated by modernity. When roots in family and community are fragile, and when traditional beliefs break down, basic human needs for connection and meaning are not met. In that context, people may turn to themselves for affirmation, rather than to others, or to society at large. Thus, narcissism is only an extreme version of that quintessential modern value, the primacy of the individual. Most people take individualism for granted. Yet it is a uniquely modern value (Nisbett, 2003), as well as a uniquely Western point of view (Markus and Kitayama, 1991; Kirmayer, 2007).

Psychotherapists also promote a highly individualistic world-view. The self is viewed as autonomous and as separate from the social fabric. Therapy sees patients as protagonists in the drama of their own lives. What it fails to take into account is the interpersonal and social context in which people live. Terms such as "self-realization" or "finding oneself" refer to an inner journey rather than an encounter with the world. Even in the modern world, it remains true that "no man is an island".

Since psychotherapy's vision so closely fits the values of the modern world, it has "trickled down" from the professional world to the culture of "pop psych". Much of the language of popular psychology is about self. There is even a "Self" magazine (mostly about fitness and diet).

The American psychologist Phillip Cushman (1995) wrote a critique of the culture of psychotherapy in which he described modern people as having an "empty self". Other people matter less if they are not a permanent part of one's life and can be easily replaced. That is why individualism leads to shallower relationships. Family and community are no longer sacred ties that must be maintained at all costs. One no longer measures self-esteem by how well one performs social tasks but by what provides personal pleasure (Kagan, 2008). Nonetheless, the culture of narcissism would not affect everyone in the same way. Only some will develop extreme levels of narcissism, while most will continue to value connection—even if they are more likely to "bowl alone".

Individualism is not absent from traditional societies but takes a different form that places it within a set of socially sanctioned options (Kirmayer, 2004). Individualism may not be associated with narcissism if conformity is socially enforced and if individuals who refuse to conform have to leave. In contrast, modern societies celebrate individuality and even allow people to be "famous for being famous". Or, in the bon mot of the painter Andy Warhol, "everyone will be famous for fifteen minutes".

Empirical data shows that cultural mechanisms can modify modal personality profiles associated with specific societies (Costa and Widiger, 2001). While there has been no research on variability in narcissism across cultures, one would expect it to be more common in some societies than in others. It would be surprising, for example, if it were as prevalent in a more traditional culture (such as Japan) as in an ultra-modern environment (such as the United States).

One of the few studies to address the question was conducted at a business school to assess the marketing of products in different countries (Durvasula et al., 2001). In Western culture, advertising constantly appeals to consumer narcissism. The researchers developed a "Vanity Scale", which they administered to samples in the United States, New Zealand, India, and China. They found that subjects in India and China were less concerned about their physical appearance or their achievements than those living in the United States or New Zealand. As globalization proceeds, these differences might eventually disappear.

Is narcissism increasing over time?

Are narcissistic traits becoming more common? Twenge and Campbell (2009) have argued strongly in support of this thesis. To examine the question, they used the narcissistic personality inventory (NPI), a self-report instrument that is standard in psychology (Raskin and Terry, 1988). Like most questionnaires, it consists of a series of items describing how people think about themselves, which are then rated on a scale ranging from "strongly agree" to "strongly disagree". However, the use of questionnaires to measure personality can suffer from discrepancies between self-reports and actual behavior. The problem might be even more severe for a trait like narcissism that interferes with accurate self-observation. Another limitation is that most studies have been conducted on university students (who are readily available but may or may not be representative of the larger population).

Twenge (2006), using data collected over several decades at a large American university, reported that NPI scores steadily rose in students since the 1980s. Twenge and Foster (2010) have published meta-analytic data supporting these conclusions. Another publication (DeWall et al., 2011) examined the linguistic content of popular song lyrics and found that narcissistic themes have been increasing, particularly after 2000. A meta-analytic study by Konrath et al. (2011) found that self-reported empathy among university students has been decreasing over the last several decades.

These findings are clearly on to something, but the conclusions need to be tempered. For example, the research does not take into account differences between ethnic groups. First-generation immigrants who have not yet acculturated to Western culture have lower levels of narcissistic traits, as shown by comparing NPI scores in immigrants to the native-born (Twenge and Foster, 2008). A contradictory study (Trzesniewski et al., 2008) was conducted at another college that attracts immigrant students who are less narcissistic. Twenge (2011) acknowledges this point, but argues that her findings hold up for the majority. What is needed are surveys that examine narcissistic traits over time in the general population, not just in university students. That research has not yet been conducted.

Finally, we do not know what NPI scores would have been like in earlier decades. Studies measuring individualism (rather than narcissism) found scores increasing in the 1960s, but leveling off in the 1980s (Roberts and Helson, 1997). This is a very complex issue. And there are other confounders. Miller and Campbell (2008) found that NPI scores are higher in men than women and that narcissism declines with age.

Twenge (2011) continues to interpret her results as reflecting cultural change, and she is probably right. She is concerned that narcissism has become a serious social problem, affecting the health of both individuals and families. I agree, but suspect that she has considered too narrow a time scale and has over-interpreted her data. Thus, the claim (Twenge and Campbell, 2009) that Americans are facing an "epidemic" of narcissism is overdrawn. Narcissism may be on the increase, but this need not be a phenomenon over recent decades, but a long-standing trend that goes back to the very birth of modernity.

Some evidence suggests that psychological symptoms that tend to be associated with narcissism are in decline. As noted in Chapter 5, indicators of social distress such as suicide (Morrell et al., 2007, Biddle et al., 2008) and substance abuse (Grant et al., 2004) have leveled off in the last decade. Even the divorce rate is down. It is hard to believe that people have suddenly become *less* narcissistic. More likely, countervailing cultural forces have come into play to mediate the effects of social change. Either modern society is not so bad or people are just getting used to it.

Self-esteem and narcissism

Maslow (1943) introduced the concept of *self-esteem* to clinical psychology. Rosenberg (1965) developed a widely used research scale to measure it. Nathaniel Branden (1969), a psychologist (and protégé of Ayn Rand), popularized this concept in several books. Self-esteem has become a buzz-word and a cliché. Under the influence of the media, many people now explain psychological problems (and bad behavior) as a consequence of their "low self-esteem".

People do need to feel good about themselves. But a positive opinion of self should not depend on entitlements or on hopes and dreams. It must be rooted in real accomplishments. Genuine self-esteem is based on a realistic appraisal of strengths and weaknesses. You don't have to be great or special, just "good enough". And if you think the world owes you success and admiration, you could be in for a come-uppance.

Thus, self-esteem is not a "thing" that people who are unhappy need more of. Having a low opinion of oneself is not the cause of psychological problems, but their *consequence*. If you are chronically unemployed, you *should* feel bad about that, and the feeling could motivate you to get a job (or go to school to prepare for one). If you have no friends or social life, you need to find a better way to connect with people. It is true that some people undervalue themselves in spite of objective achievements. In such cases, therapists can work to correct these misperceptions. But I see too many patients who over-value themselves and blame others for their failures.

Self-esteem is not a skill that should be taught in schools (Hewitt, 1998; Hunter, 2000). As noted by Twenge and Campbell (2009), the current idea that teaching children to value themselves should be part of a school curriculum is very mistaken. This idea says more about American "boosterism" than about science. Education does help people to have a sense of worth—by teaching them skills on which self-esteem could be based. But it need not offer courses on how to feel better without accomplishing anything. Moreover, the idea that raising self-esteem makes people value themselves or makes them happier and more effective in life has no scientific basis.

In summary, self-esteem does not develop *de novo*. It is socially embedded, based on real accomplishments in a real world that are acknowledged by others. We can think well of ourselves if we work well and love well. But if the only basis for self-esteem lies inside the mind, it is little but narcissism in disguise.

Psychotherapy and self-esteem

The idea that psychotherapy should raise self-esteem is often taken for granted, but it is fundamentally mistaken. Too much focus on this goal can make treatment go wrong. When therapy goes well, and when patients learn to function better, self-esteem follows naturally. It is a consequence, not a precondition of psychological change.

Psychotherapy need not be an exciting inner voyage, which the rest of the world needs to accommodate. Rather, it is a means to an end of social competence. Psychotherapy can teach people that success in intimate relationships or in a career is difficult and requires many hard compromises. Later in this book, I will discuss that process under the rubric of "getting a life". People who succeed in that goal will also gain self-esteem.

By and large, people with high levels of narcissistic traits need to *lower* their self-esteem, not to raise it. In therapy, they need tactful confrontations to show the consequences of being arrogant and insensitive. And guilt is not a bad thing if you have something to feel guilty about (That is why Alcoholics Anonymous has always advised people in recovery to "make amends" to everyone they have hurt.).

One can have high self-esteem and still be quite dysfunctional. Research shows that criminals score high on self-esteem (Baumeister et al., 1996). They think well of themselves because they do not care about anyone else, and think they have the right to do anything they want. People who have an excessively high (and unjustified) opinion of themselves treat others badly, as a result of which their lives go badly as well.

These principles have implications for the conduct of psychotherapy. An approach that is overly sympathetic to personal needs is unlikely to make a dent in well-entrenched narcissistic attitudes. In such cases, raising self-esteem will be more of a problem than a solution.

A hotel I recently stayed in advertised itself: "why settle for the ordinary?" My reaction was to wonder "why not?" Do we really want to live in a culture in which every experience has to be extraordinary, every relationship has to be passionate, and every job has to be fulfilling? We have lost sight of the ordinary, and more sustaining, aspects of our lives. Human beings have always lived in societies. There never has been such a thing as an individual outside of a social context. Social relationships are not imposed on us but are embedded in our identity and in the structure of our minds (Pinker, 2002).

Antidotes to narcissism

Modernity is a Faustian bargain. It offers us freedom at the price of alienation. But we cannot go back to a traditional way of life—nor should we even try.

Attachment to a cause beyond the self is the best antidote to narcissism. Young people today are as idealistic as their predecessors. Every generation has its cause, in which youth takes the lead. Today's issue is the environment, providing many young people with a larger and more inspiring commitment than self. But while modern youth still makes commitments, it takes a boutique approach. Instead of buying a whole package (such as that offered over many centuries by organized religion), they pick the causes they *choose* to be concerned about.

Most people will sacrifice self for a community to which they feel strongly attached. Social networks and social loyalties are based on the principle of *reciprocal altruism*, the expectation that if one gives, one can expect to receive at a later time. All societies function on this basis. In the long run, people who "cheat" others and fail to follow the rules are brought into check by negative reinforcements and social controls (Tooby and Cosmides 1990). Social arrangements allow for meeting personal needs while reinforcing cooperation (Wright, 2000).

We are all taught as children to feel guilty (or at least ashamed) when fairness and reciprocity are not respected. Modern people often think of guilt as a problem, as do psychotherapists. Yet remorse is one of the forces that preserve social order. With the decline of guilt, and in the absence of common values about right and wrong, modernity produces moral relativism. Some people no longer grant anyone else the right to dictate standards of behavior. And the relation of the individual to society has come to be more shaped by rights than by responsibilities.

Psychotherapy has an intrinsic tendency to decrease guilt. As the Catholic Church has long known, talking to an understanding listener reduces the sense of sin. Patients who admit their misbehaviors and are met with understanding (rather than judgment) usually feel better. By and large, therapists are trained to take a somewhat permissive view of every action. If you do something wrong, you may be caught, but your therapist is unlikely to censure you. For people who are not particularly narcissistic, that process can be helpful. But for those who have a strong sense of entitlement, it tends to be counter-productive.

Therapists are not supposed to tell people how to live. Freud thought it axiomatic that the job of a therapist is to free a patient from the bonds of "neurosis"—after which life choices can be made more "freely". But being strictly non-judgmental is also rooted in values. Therapists need not take the view that almost any action or life choice (short of criminal behavior) is acceptable if it makes the individual happier.

Even if they pretend to be neutral, therapists have many ways of letting their preferences be known. Comments to patients may be subtle but are usually far from non-judgmental. Values in psychotherapy are not delivered *ex cathedra* but are implicit. But therapists are often too afraid of straight talk. Some tie themselves into knots (albeit elegant knots) with circumlocutions. Tact is a virtue, but patients also need to hear criticism. The trick is to get patients to listen without making them angry and defensive.

We live in a society where criticizing the actions of others can bring suspicion on those who dare to condemn them. The question that is often asked is: "what right do *you* have to judge?" While psychotherapists usually try to steer clear of ethical issues, the clinical encounter is shaped by values. Whether a patient's values reflect tradition or cultural narcissism, therapists need to consider the outcome—for individuals and for society at large.

Therapists may be hesitant to give advice, a principle that makes sense when you know that some people tend to resist even the most well-intentioned suggestions. But it does not follow that one should express no opinion at all about what is right or wrong. And in the long run, patients in therapy cannot get well without being committed to something outside the self.

The problem is that the therapeutic method itself has a strong intrinsic tendency to reinforce narcissism. That is a problem that affects *all* forms of psychotherapy, and is not particular to any one technique. Most people enter therapy because of a failure in close relationships (Westen, 1998). Exploring the recesses of the self is not necessarily the best way to address these problems. Therapy is not a technical "fix" to allow people to get what they want out of life. Choices have to be made and expectations have to be realistic.

An old saying (attributed to the American journalist Sydney J. Harris) is: "If you're not part of the solution, you're part of the problem." Talking therapy is not good at combating cultural narcissism and often ends up supporting it. But psychotherapy must stand aside from the culture that created it. It can take a perspective that might be called *anti-narcissistic.* Therapists need to help patients look outward, not just inward.

7
Therapy Culture

Psychotherapy is more than a treatment. It is a *weltanschauung*—a point of view on the world. As WH Auden (1939/1979) wrote in his elegy on the death of Freud, "for us, he has now become, not a person, but a climate of opinion".

Talking therapy, a product of modern culture, has greatly affected that culture in return. In a rapidly changing world, a belief emerged that changing the psyche is sufficient to change one's life (Furedi, 2004). Therapy culture has promoted other illusions. One is the belief that boosting self-esteem is a recipe for psychological health. Another is the tendency to see people as victims of traumatic events, rather than as agents of their own resilience (Furedi, 2008).

Making emotions more important than reality works against (rather than for) social change (Moskowitz, 2001). "Therapizing" the human condition may only serve to distract people from real problems. I once asked a physician who had worked in Ethiopia whether people developed PTSD there after the famine. Her answer was, "they had no time for that".

The psychotherapist as guru

Even today, some are in awe of psychotherapists. (How many times have I heard the question: "Oh, you're a psychiatrist—can you read my mind?") These attitudes reflect, in part, the fact that we are all afraid of losing our minds. Mental healers are both feared and respected because they are sanctioned with the power to define sanity.

Moreover, the belief that psychotherapists have a key to the unconscious mind makes them even more fearsome as shamans. That is why the arts have taken such a strong interest in the drama of therapy. Several novels have been written in which a plot turns on repression, and the cinema has often made use of that dramatic twist (Gabbard and Gabbard, 1999). For many years, mental health professionals have been asked to pontificate on all kinds of subjects, from politics to the right way of bringing up children (Paris, 2005). In this way, therapists were asked to function as secular priests—for a society that lost its faith. Therapy culture has made clinicians act like gurus.

In the past, religious leaders conducted services in houses of worship, where they advised their parishioners about issues of the day. And they were not shy about telling people how to live. Moreover, religious leaders were expected to live exemplary lives that would inspire members of their congregations to follow suit. These behaviors remain characteristic of fundamentalist groups but not of mainstream churches. While popes still make pronouncements on social issues, Catholics in Western countries often ignore them. By and large, fewer people look to ministers and priests to tell them how to live their lives (Norris and Ingelhardt, 2004). Yet the need for personal guidance has not gone away. For some, that niche has been filled by psychotherapy (North, 1972).

But how much do therapists actually know about life? Their professional experience makes them experts on psychological symptoms. But do they know how to function in society? It is one thing to understand mental illness, and quite another to know the secret of happiness and fulfillment.

Second, as churches have long recognized, anyone who tells other people how to live had better have a blameless life. People who are suspicious of psychotherapists sometimes take pleasure in discovering their limitations as spouses or parents. Actually, research shows that the ability of therapists to manage their own lives is no better (but no worse) than anyone else's (Beutler et al., 2003).

The obvious conclusion is that therapists should stick to their job and stop pontificating. But since having your opinion requested is flattering, pontification has had a long history. Therapists have sometimes been asked to write advice columns in newspapers and magazines. I can remember one that ran for many years in the local paper when I was growing up. Authored by Rose Franzblau, a psychologist trained in psychoanalysis, it strongly promoted the traditional family, and advised nearly everyone who wrote in to seek therapy.

The idea that psychotherapists know how children should be raised has been widely accepted in our culture. Yet in spite of Benjamin Spock (1998), and more recent authors on the subject, there is little science behind the many volumes of advice to parents on child care. Researchers have not conducted the kind of studies that could provide real guidance.

By and large, we know more about how parents can ruin children than how they should raise them. One of the characteristics of modern life is that many life decisions have been professionalized in a way that makes people feel fearful and inadequate, and this is one of the problematic side effects of psychotherapy (Sommers and Satel, 2005). As Furedi (2008) notes, professionalization of expertise in child rearing undermines the judgment of parents, making them "paranoid" about all the supposed dangers of ruining their children.

At least one prominent "expert" on child care turned out to be highly suspect. Bruno Bettelheim, an Austrian-born psychoanalyst who ran a school for disturbed children in Chicago, was a major cultural figure in the 1960s. For many years his advice on child rearing, published in the *Ladies Home Journal*, was taken very seriously by the general public. But after his death, a biographer (Pollak, 1998) exposed Bettelheim as a fraud (false claims about his training and his treatment of disturbed children, plagiarism in his books, and sadistic beating of children under his care). People should have known better. Needless to say, Bettelheim's views on how to raise children were based on personal opinions, not on scientific findings.

Some psychotherapists present themselves as experts on romantic love. Erich Fromm, a German psychologist who later lived in the United States and Mexico, was a neo-Freudian analyst and lifelong socialist who wrote best-selling books about totalitarianism, war, and peace. A formidable cultural icon of the post-war era, Fromm was read by millions. (I remember a group hanging on his every word at the 1971 meeting of the World Psychiatric Association in Mexico City.)

In his most popular book, *The Art of Loving*, Fromm (1956) defined the differences between healthy and neurotic affection. The most essential point, which has since become a cliché, is that you cannot love another person without loving yourself first. Otherwise love is little but emotional neediness.

Even if this advice were credible, Fromm's book consisted of rhetoric masquerading as profundity. Self-love is no guarantee of anything. If you love yourself, you might prefer focusing on your own needs rather than meeting those of another person. And as one reviewer at the time remarked archly about this book, Fromm must have known a lot about love—after being married four times.

Psychotherapy and values

While Freud was a cultural conservative, as psychoanalysis found a strong base in the United States, it absorbed modernity and American values. In the "therapeutic culture" described by Rieff (1966), actions are judged by motivations rather than by consequences. Individualism and a consumer culture also appeal to the need for displaying one's assets—as opposed to values based on connection and service (Miller, 2009). In this way, the culture of therapy became a culture of narcissism.

The idea that self-love is a good thing was the banner of the generation that came of age in the 1960s. Young people revolted against conventional love and marriage, and the spirit rejection is far from extinguished. But these ideas have not led to any increase in human happiness. On the contrary, the rejection of social structures in which loving feelings can be expressed has created a new cultural problem.

In the 1960s and 1970s, Fritz Perls, a German–American psychologist trained as a psychoanalyst, developed a method called "gestalt therapy" (Perls, 1969), and became one of the first "new age" therapists. He promoted an active, directive method that focused on experience in the present moment (particularly in the therapist–client relationship). Toward the end of his life, Perls was involved in a program of weekend "encounter groups" sponsored by the Esalen Institute in Big Sur, California. This kind of therapy became famous, in part because it sometimes encouraged partner swapping or frank promiscuity (as satirized in the 1969 film *Bob and Carol and Ted and Alice*).

The focus of Perls' approach was on the self, with commitments and relationships taking a distant second place. (He was also known for having sex with clients.) Perls became a cult figure, in part due to the "Fritz Perls Poster" that could be found on many walls of the apartments of the young. The poster provided an attractive scene from nature accompanied by these words:

> I do my thing, and you do your thing.
> I am not in this world to live up to your expectations,
> And you are not in this world to live up to mine.
> You are you and I am I;
> If by chance we find each other, it's beautiful.
> If not, it can't be helped.

These sentiments sum up the essence of cultural narcissism. The poster's philosophy idealizes brief encounters and one-night stands. It contains not one word about commitment to anything beyond the self. That these ideas were ever taken seriously says volumes about therapy culture. And some of our patients live by these principles, even if sex does little for their failure to connect to other people.

As psychotherapy moved out of the consulting room and came to play an important role in setting standards for social values, several commentators began to criticize the tendency to psychologize every issue facing modern society (Gross, 1978). Therapy culture is not particularly therapeutic for society. It undermines traditional social values without offering anything substantial to replace them.

Psychotherapy and moral responsibility

When religious ideas dominated Western society, people could (and did) talk comfortably and frequently about "sin". Today that word seems impossibly moralistic. If people no longer believe in any absolute standard for behavior, then the only sin lies in failing to obtain pleasure for oneself. The reluctance to hold people accountable for their actions is reflected in therapy culture.

The language we use to describe bad behavior places us squarely in the world of Rieff's (1966) "psychological man". Bad conduct is only "dysfunctional" (a comment on consequences) or "inappropriate" (a comment on social expectations)—but not necessarily "wrong". We prefer to see people not as evil or sinful but as troubled and in need of therapeutic guidance.

The idea that moral responsibility is obsolete fits with the assumption that the way you *feel* is more important than the way you *act* (Furedi, 2008). If circumstances make you feel bad about yourself, you cannot be blamed for behaving badly. Even social problems have been open to the same analysis. Thus, people might not just be poor but suffer from low self-esteem. (If they were rich, their self-esteem would no doubt increase lock-step with their income.)

Based on these ideas, judges have been known to *sentence* people convicted of crimes to undergo psychotherapy. Lawyers have often argued in court that their clients should be let off if they can be proved to suffer from a psychiatric diagnosis, most often when the courts are asked to deal with crimes that do not seriously challenge public safety. The main example is sexual exhibitionism, but there is no evidence that forced treatment for sexual disorders is effective (Laws and O'Donohue, 1997). Some of the same issues arise in civil actions, such as custody disputes or child protection. Parents may be asked to see therapists if the court thinks they are harming their children. But there is no evidence that psychotherapy makes people better equipped to be parents.

Sometimes ethical issues arise *directly* in the course of therapy. While clinicians try to understand, they are sometimes forced to disapprove.

For example, one of the accepted exceptions to confidentiality in therapy involves situations where a child is seen to be at risk. At the very least, therapists are expected to ask patients to give up behaviors that are harmful to innocent parties or to report child abuse to the authorities (Slovenko, 1998).

Psychological treatment is not a drug that normalizes those who take it. Talking therapy cannot be mandated; it requires a personal commitment to change.

Psychotherapy and sexual freedom

Psychotherapy began by being socially subversive. That was most striking in relation to sexual behavior. Freud (1930/1989) supported sexual freedom and thought that repression causes neurotic symptoms. The needs of the individual for pleasure were seen as valid, while the idea that sexuality can be a threat to the social fabric was downplayed.

Cultural anthropologists often took the same view. After the First World War, when sexual mores were changing rapidly, the anthropologist Margaret Mead (1928/2001) wrote a best-selling book claiming that pre-marital sex was universal among Samoan adolescents. Her agenda was to encourage young Americans to act the same way. Actually, Mead's claims turned out to be bogus—she knew little about Samoan culture, did not speak the language, and heard what she wanted to hear from informants. Freeman (1983), who worked there for years (not months), found that Samoa was (and still is) a society in which traditional values are dominant. But Mead's book appealed to its American readers, who no longer believed in the legitimacy of sexual restriction.

In many traditional societies, sex outside marriage (particularly for women) has been seen as a threat to the integrity of the family and of society. And so it was—until reliable contraception removed most of the consequences. The obvious exception is sexually transmitted infections—but needless to say, contraception has not eliminated the birth of unwanted children.

The period following the end of the First World War was the true watershed for changes in sexual behavior (Laumann et al., 1994). Although many people think of the 1960s as the time when a "sexual revolution" occurred, all that actually happened was that "free love" came out in the open. Pre-marital sexual intercourse was already common in the 1920s. (Couples willing to wait until the wedding came mainly from the upper classes.) Women were no longer closely supervised to keep them chaste, and most men no longer expected their wives to be virginal. While the birth control pill had not yet been developed, other reliable ways of preventing pregnancy were widely available.

The First World War had a profound effect on Western society (Eksteins, 1989). The slaughter of war made people skeptical of authority and, once it was over, some focused more on pleasure than on duty. Thus, the 1920s marked the true end of Victorian morality. Yet changes in sexual behavior were not always openly talked about. When the Kinsey reports came out (Kinsey et al., 1948, 1953), many were surprised to learn the extent to which traditional mores had already been eroded. There was vigorous discussion in the media at the time about whether to believe Kinsey's findings. And his numbers were indeed exaggerated (there were serious sampling problems). Yet in essence, Kinsey was right. By the 1940s, only a minority entered marriage without previous sexual experience—and quite a large percentage failed to remain faithful afterwards.

Even though Freud believed in a free sexual life, he did not live that way himself. And as psychoanalysis moved into the mainstream, its perspective became more conservative. Analysts often supported family values; it was not (and still is not) unusual for extramarital affairs to be seen as symptoms. In this way, some psychotherapists became arbiters of conventional morality. But it is irrational to condemn adultery wholesale. There can be many different reasons for sexual affairs, and not all of them break up families.

The other side of the coin was the idealization of sexuality as an end in itself. Wilhelm Reich, an Austrian-born renegade psychoanalyst (and early "new age" therapist) placed the capacity for orgasm at the center of human psychology (Sharaf, 1983). Reich was an eccentric and grandiose man who thought he had made a great scientific discovery (and believed that flying saucers were spying on him to find out about it). Reich died in prison, after being prosecuted in the 1950s for selling "orgone boxes", the wooden cases that he claimed drew on some universal energy. While Reich's ideas died out, he was part of a trend in which sex took on an almost mystical significance. It was not a far journey from these ideas to the hedonism promoted by the best-selling book *The Joy of Sex* (Comfort, 1972).

Psychotherapy has always been influenced by prevailing cultural trends and has never been value-free—either when promoting sexual freedom or when suggesting that sexual activity needs to be socially controlled. Hardly anyone today (outside traditional religions) challenges the current consensus that unmarried people can have an active sex life. The problem for moderns is whether they view sex as a simple erotic release (in which case, 'the more the better"), or whether sex serves as bonding behavior (in which case, sexual promiscuity can indeed be a problem). Support for the latter view comes from community surveys showing that unusually high levels of sexual activity correlate with *lower*, not higher levels of mental health (Langstrom and Hanson, 2006).

The culture of blame

Nobody guarantees children contented and empathic parents. In the course of human history, most people grew up with much less support than the average family provides today. (It was only when I took up psychiatry as a profession that I realized that my own family, for all its faults, was well within the normal range.)

Even if your parents don't understand your feelings, nothing prevents you from finding other people who do. Of course, some parents do deserve blame. When caretakers are alcoholic and violently abusive, children suffer an increased risk for psychopathology (Rutter and Rutter 1993). But that is different from more subtle failings, such as a lack of ability to understand a child's feelings. The idea that parents who are unempathic do permanent damage to their children is an unproven hypothesis that has sometimes been used to blame families for psychological problems. And sometimes, as in recovered memory therapy, the blame process can become malignant.

The average family may be far from ideal, but parents have been given a "bad rap" by therapy culture (Furedi, 2008). By and large, most parents try their best, and deficits are on the subtle side. In any case, one cannot *always* understand children. Moreover, children have other reasons for developing psychological problems, some deriving from temperament, others deriving from the social environment (Harris, 2006).

The idea that psychological problems are due to parental maltreatment or misunderstanding was a core belief in psychoanalytic psychotherapy. I was trained to think that way by my teachers. This kind of "formulation" was an exercise that I learned to master during residency (at a time when Freudian ideas dominated psychiatry), and I learned how to play on this instrument like a virtuoso. The procedure is simple (Cardoso-Zoppe et al., 2009). You observe conflicts in current life experiences and find parallels in the patient's childhood. (If you look hard enough, you can always find something.) *Ipso facto*, the latter is formulated as the cause of the former.

It took many years for me to understand why this exercise is a fallacy. I eventually wrote a book (Paris, 2000) to help others avoid reaching such conclusions. Parent-blaming, like other attributions, offers only the illusion of an explanation. It does not even do justice to the experience of childhood, given that children are only *relatively* (not absolutely) powerless.

In summary, people are not unhappy because their parents did not love them sufficiently. Is it ever possible to love children enough? Those of us who have raised our own children know that the answer is *no*. "Good enough", not perfect, should be the standard.

A large number of people who have had problematic childhoods do perfectly well as adults (Paris, 2000). When serious psychological problems start early, one gets the impression that an unhappy childhood is a cause but can also be an effect (Rutter and Rutter, 1993). In other words, when things start badly, they tend to remain bad, and vicious cycles can develop. By and large, childhood adversities increase the risk for psychopathology—but only on a *statistical* basis. Resilience is the rule, not the exception.

Children are resilient because they have to be. Parents have to be consistently malignant to hurt them in any permanent way. Most of the time, we do not really know what makes some children grow up troubled while others muddle through or thrive. And when people feel better, they can stop blaming their families and spend time with them without feeling the sensitivity of a child.

As the stance of blame spread into therapy culture, parents were made over-anxious about harming their children (Furedi, 2008). Some have even become afraid to discipline or criticize children due to the fear that doing so might turn out to be "traumatic". Some have even been reluctant to send their children to day care, for fear of interfering with the attachment process. Actually, research shows that differences between children in and out of day care are too small to be of clinical significance (Belsky et al., 2007). Moreover, there is very good evidence that children throughout history have usually been raised by many caretakers, not one mother alone (Hrdy, 2009).

The blaming of parents, rooted in therapy culture, provides adults with unhelpful excuses. Patients in talking therapy can spend years exploring their childhood and inner feelings, and do little or nothing about their present life. They can go on for years detailing every injury, large or small, that one has endured. Even if we all have an "inner child", we do not need to listen to it. (Some wags have even suggested that an inner child can benefit from being sent to its room.)

The recovery and self-help movements have long promulgated a dogma of parental blame (Kaminer, 1992). The principle that "dysfunctional families" are crippling is widely accepted. And some therapists have encouraged false memories of child abuse, which are then used to account for every psychological problem under the sun (McNally, 2003).

Psychotherapy is ultimately a story—not a scientific procedure but a narrative. It is not an accurate exploration of life history. Yet treating the past as the key determinant of current experience *seems* to offer a meaningful narrative. This historical point of view creates a paradox. The rights and wrongs of the present can be influenced by the past but are not *determined* by it. A more productive approach to psychotherapy could be based on the famous quip: "This is the first day of the rest of your life."

While effective psychotherapy is always oriented to the future, clinicians know that change is difficult. As Alcoholics Anonymous famously put it, recovery occurs "one day at a time". But even the worst turns of fate allow for freedom to improve quality of life. One need only ask therapists who work with the chronically ill or in palliative care for the dying. In the end, explaining current problems on the basis of the past is illusory. These attributions are no more scientific than the idea that psychological symptoms are caused by witchcraft.

The cult of the victim

Blaming others makes it easier to feel like a victim. To move beyond a closed circle of self, people need to become responsible for their own lives.

The ethos of talking therapy has encouraged people to see themselves as a victim of childhood experiences and past traumas. Therapeutic narratives that focus on an injured self create a perception of having innocently suffered from the actions of others. This rarely raises one's quality of life. Instead, it tends to confirm one's status as victim, converting personal narratives into sacred texts (Dineen, 1996; Sykes, 1992).

The drama of personal victimization has been widely played out in the media. Stories of trauma invite us to feel sorrow, pity, and anger—rather than admire resilience to adversity. A somewhat better identity for an adult with a truly traumatic past is to be a *survivor*.

Even in psychotherapy, talking about the past is not always the best way to spend precious time. Needless to say, psychotherapists must always understand what their patients have gone through and "bear witness" to their sorrows. Having someone "feel your pain" can be an important first step for helping people who have long felt misunderstood and invalidated. But that does not mean that patients need to spend *most* of the time in therapy talking about childhood experiences. While most of us experience helpless feelings as children, we grow into adults who have choices and can choose to live differently.

The past does cast a shadow on the present. Research confirms the principle that past experiences make us more sensitive to situations that remind us of earlier difficulties (Rutter and Rutter, 1993). But these relationships are more complicated than most therapists think. For example, past experiences can lead people to *choose* situations that are similar to the past or to provoke others to behave in the same way.

Once understood, such patterns can be modified. No matter how difficult the past has been, there is no reason to remain in a victim role. Too much of a focus on past suffering encourages self-absorption and a sense of entitlement in the present.

Research has documented a relationship between taking a victim role and narcissistic personality traits (McCullough et al., 2003). This makes sense, since self-regard can be supported by blame. Yet a wide body of research shows that when something traumatic happens, people need (as much as possible) to take control of the situation (Hayes et al., 1999). One need not be mired in the past if there are options in the present.

Several aspects of modern culture have encouraged people to take on the victim role. Entire groups have claimed to become "empowered" by proclaiming their injuries (Dineen, 1996). Autobiographies, which used to tell stories about conquering adversity through persistence and hard work, may now focus on the impact of childhood trauma. Yet even people who have been subjected to the worst experiences (such as concentration camps) can rise above them and begin life again (McNally, 2003). It is fortunate that human beings are resilient. If they were not, our species might have never survived.

Paradoxically, the status of victim can give some people an identity and a purpose (Sykes, 1992). Experienced psychotherapists begin by validating these perceptions, but must encourage patients to move on. The principle is that people need to "own" their problems. Otherwise, much like a traditional religious person invoking "God's will", they may feel paralyzed by fate.

The dialectic that drives therapy is to validate people's life experiences—and then ask them to change (Linehan, 1993). The process need not be disempowering. What I like to say to patients is, "You have had a difficult time. But nothing prevents you now from making your life better."

The language of therapy culture

One of the most telling aspects of therapy culture is the way it uses words. The purpose is not necessarily to communicate ideas. Rather, language functions as a signal to others that one is thinking psychologically. Furedi (2004) has documented how "buzz-words" such as self-esteem and trauma now appear frequently in the popular media.

The American journalist Richard Rosen (1977) labeled this phenomenon "psychobabble". The terminology impresses, even if it fails to shed much light on anything. Actually, words don't matter as long as you let everyone see that you are up to date with therapy culture. How people talk about themselves (and other people) has been influenced by psychological ideas. We may have a slip of the tongue and say, "I didn't mean that *consciously*". We may examine our dreams for clues to the unconscious mind.

In the heyday of psychoanalysis, several of its favorite terms found their way into common parlance. People were described as "conflicted" or "fixated". Or, borrowing a phrase from the Austrian psychologist Alfred Adler, they may suffer from an "inferiority complex".

The current invocation of low self-esteem to explain all kinds of misbehavior is only the latest version of psychobabble. Politicians have sometimes excused extramarital affairs as a consequence of "narcissism". In this way, moral judgments are replaced by psychological explanations. Even though most people have never been in psychotherapy, they may think about life as if they were. In other words, the inner world becomes more important than the outside world.

In popular psychology, buzz-words give an impression of understanding. One of the most prominent examples is "self-esteem". Another popular phrase that doesn't explain much is the concept of a "dysfunctional family" (Kaminer, 1992). While I sometimes find myself using this term as a shorthand, in common parlance it has become little more than a cliché that doesn't explain what aspect of family functioning is impaired, or why.

"Codependency" is another coinage from the recovery movement (Kaminer, 1992). This buzz-word carries the implication that people who behave badly are helped to do so by intimates. But it doesn't tell you what determines why a partner chooses to live with a substance abuser (or just leave).

"Denial", a term borrowed from psychoanalysis, has been used to describe almost any situation in which people don't accept reality. While some forms of psychological blindness can be defense mechanisms, this word should not be used automatically to describe people who refuse to see the world in the same way as we do.

Any influential set of ideas, once it becomes part of popular culture, can be vulgarized. But behind the fast and easy use of psychological terms lies another problem. The idea is that to be happy, all we need to do is put our dysfunctional family behind us, put a stop to our denial and codependency, and raise our self-esteem. It is all too glib, and all too easy.

Therapy culture and privacy

The values of therapy culture are also associated with a shift in the traditional standards of privacy. Furedi (2004) has described these trends in detail—and he was writing before the golden age of blogs.

Throughout most of history, there have been things most people would and would not talk about. (Now and then, most of them had to do with sex.) But in psychotherapy, you are *supposed* to reveal everything. Every detail of your sex life can be shared with a therapist. This radical openness is no longer confined to therapy sessions, but has become part of modern media culture. People can reveal their deepest secrets in public—as if they were in treatment. In "confessional television", people tell you more than you want to know about themselves and their personal lives". It is as if psychotherapy, once the sacred sanctum of privacy, is being conducted in front of an audience of millions. Some of these confessions are widely distributed on the Internet. It does not even hurt celebrities to circulate videos showing them having sex, if that makes them "famous for being famous".

Thus, the sense of shame that once kept intimate matters private has changed. There was a time when only therapists knew about your sex life. This is not the case any more. The media can strip anyone naked, and in this way it is dangerous to be famous. Politicians, whose love affairs were traditionally kept under wraps, no longer have private lives. Biographies, once circumspect and idealizing, have turned into tell-all "pathographies". In the media, little about life remains behind a wall of privacy.

The loss of privacy also has roots in narcissistic self-display. In a remark attributed to the Irish writer (and famous narcissist) Oscar Wilde, "There is only one thing in life worse than being talked about, and that is not being talked about." In any case, society no longer values stoicism (Lloyd, 2008). In a world where personal interests predominate, the pursuit of pleasure and the expression of feelings are more important than bearing suffering with dignity. It may be accepted that everyone should let feelings "hang out", as one does in therapy. Dealing with problems without complaining is evidently outdated.

That point of view is not confined to the consulting room. The belief is current that when something bad happens, what people need to do above all is to *talk* (Showalter, 1997). That idea has survived scientific evidence to the contrary, which shows that most people would do better to not seek treatment directly following a traumatic experience, but take the time to work things out in their mind first (McNally, 2003). For many years, it has been customary to assume that people who survive traumas (such as students after a school shooting) need to be counseled using a method called "critical incident debriefing" (Mitchell, 1983). In fact, research has consistently shown that intruding on private grief in that way makes people feel worse, not better (Sijbrandji et al., 2006). Yet one still hears after almost every disastrous event that counselors, like the cavalry in a classical Western movie, are on the way.

Behind all these trends lies individualism and, its stepchild, narcissism. The modern focus on personal needs, and on the primacy of romantic love, has failed to solve the problems of modern alienation. People still need to attach, connect, and belong to something larger than the self. Many people in modern world are trapped in a feedback loop—talking *to* themselves instead of building links to a wider world.

Giving responsible psychotherapy a voice

In therapy culture, the voices that are most heard are not always the most responsible ones. Many prominent psychotherapists in our culture have been seekers after celebrity. Phil McGraw, the popular "Dr. Phil" of American television fame, had his license to practice therapy taken away but still manages to earn millions because of his unique talents as a communicator (Dembling, 2005). McGraw's cliché-ridden approach to raising self-esteem has been praised by other celebrities, even if it has no basis in science.

In contrast, responsible therapists do *not* usually go on television. They are more interested in helping patients. They keep up with the scientific literature, work hard to improve their practice, and do not make pronouncements on subjects they know little about. They stay out of the public eye and concentrate on helping people in distress. For this reason, responsible clinicians are not always heard. The dominant voices are those of marketers who have something to sell.

Psychotherapists should inform the public that they practice an evidence-based method (assuming, of course, that they do). The most useful methods of talking therapy have never been part of therapy culture. In the long run, the truth could win out.

Part III

Practice

8
Sustaining the Family

Why the family is universal

Human universals are cultural patterns common to all societies (Murdock, 1949; Brown, 1991). The most prominent is the family. While variations in its structure can be found, families have existed in all cultures and throughout human history (Shorter, 1977).

A family remains the best way to raise children. This is not a prejudice but a conclusion supported by research. A large literature shows that living in a family promotes mental health (Amato et al., 2007). There are good reasons for this relationship. Families meet emotional needs by providing intimacy and attachment; although, as we will see, these needs can be met in other ways.

To raise children, having two parents is advantageous, largely because human beings produce a small number of offsprings that take many years to reach maturity. Parental care requires commitment, and humans are programmed for kin selection so that shared genes promote altruistic behavior (Barkow, Cosmides and Tooby, 1992).

While there are other options, most people live in nuclear rather than in extended families. By and large, families that function well promote mental health, while broken or problematic families increase the risk for psychological symptoms (Reder, McClure, and Jolley, 2000). In general, the maintenance of family structure is good for children, while anything that undermines that structure is bad for them (Amato and Booth, 1997). The main exception concerns situations of family violence and serious substance abuse, in which children can benefit from dissolution of a family (Rutter and Rutter, 1993). In summary, the idea that psychotherapists should work to keep most families intact is not a moral injunction. It is a clinical application of scientific data.

However, the family need not conform to what are (mistakenly) considered "traditional" patterns. In the course of history, marriage was rarely a love-match or a perpetual romance. Traditionally, it was an economic arrangement between two families. But marriage created a structure for the cooperative raising of children, and since most couples worked together, it was also an economic unit. The idea of marrying *only* for love, while always an option, did not become widely popular before the 18th century (Coontz, 2005).

The main variation on the nuclear family is the joint family, in which children also live with one set of grandparents (Shorter, 1977). Multi-generational families have the advantage of providing support for parents and multiple attachment figures for children. A few cultures have tolerated polygamy, but that option was restricted to those who could afford it. In every society, some people have remained unmarried by choice. Many cultures validate that option through defined religious vocations. There can be little doubt that some people are better off single.

Whereas establishing a family was once an intrinsic part of life in the community, today it is a matter of personal choice. The result is that some people are lonelier than ever. There are several reasons for this outcome. One is that some are not able to establish a family on their own. The decline of the arranged marriage and the rise of romantic choice mean that people may not have the skills required to find their own partners. Also, some have a problem committing to any relationship. Thus the right to choose can make the attainment of intimacy more difficult. Patients in psychotherapy often describe difficulties making these choices or suffering the consequences of wrong choices. Moreover, many have difficulty accepting the inevitable limitations of intimacy. The high divorce rate in contemporary society reflects a culture in which the individual is more important than the group. It also reflects a cultural narcissism that encourages people to want what is ideal, rather than what is realistically possible.

If living in a family is better for mental health, talking therapy should generally aim to sustain family life, help those who have not achieved successful intimacy to find it, and provide alternatives to those for whom family life is not suitable. This chapter will examine how these goals might be accomplished. Unfortunately, the very process of talking therapy can undermine rather than strengthen family relationships. That is because therapy has a strong tendency to reinforce individual and cultural narcissism. Focusing exclusively on individual needs is inimical to the negotiation and compromise that keeps families functioning.

The family under siege

Modern writers have often described the family as being "under siege" (Lasch, 1977). We need to understand the social forces that have undermined its stability.

Ever since the Enlightenment, Western culture encouraged suspicion of or rebellion against tradition and authority. In the French Revolution, the right of aristocrats to rule was overturned. Religious belief, while not eliminated, was greatly weakened. Eventually, the authority of the family also came to be questioned. Political radicals were at the forefront of the critique. The idea of "freedom" was extended from its original meaning (the overthrow of abusive governments) to rejection of any social structure that proscribed or prescribed behavior. For example, many of the founders of utopian communities in the 19th century favored free love and rejected family ties of any kind (Muncy, 1973).

Friedrich Engels, Karl Marx's collaborator, thought that the family was in no way "natural". Instead, he saw it as a unit of capitalist society that promotes oppression of women and patriarchy over children (Engels, 1884/1972). He argued for the complete abolition of this "bourgeois" institution. Not all Marxists went that far. (Karl Marx had a wife and children, although he also allowed himself a mistress.) In the 20th century, many revolutionary movements encouraged people to value political loyalty over family attachments.

Engels was right that traditional families tend to be patriarchal and to control behavior. Yet the uncomfortable truth is that patriarchy has been the norm throughout most of human history (Goldberg, 1973, 1993). (Needless to say, that need not mean we should retain patriarchy.) In the same way, authoritarian political structures have characterized most societies up to the modern era. There were reasons for subservience. When people lived in villages and had to raise crops to survive, it was better to accept authority. Patriarchy also fitted in with the need of men for status and was based on the importance of male physical strength for protecting the community and carrying out physical labor. These social roles and expectations were passed on from generation to generation.

In modern society, the patriarchal family is an anachronism. We only have to observe the presence of "honor killing" in some Islamic societies to see how oppressive these traditions can be. And in the United States, the term "family values" has come to be a code word for a conservative agenda linked to fundamentalist religion. Yet even though traditional patriarchal families, supported by religion and the community, were more stable, and even though formal divorce was uncommon before recent times, marital partners have not always stayed together. Men could simply go away and never return. Abandoned women had to find a way to survive. And the abandonment of children by mothers was also common: it is well documented as late as the 18th and 19th centuries (Shorter, 1977) and still occurs.

The traditional family is associated with rural life, while the contemporary family is a product of urbanization and modernity. Patriarchy is no longer necessary when most people live in cities and do not need to worry about their physical survival. In cities, young people can also take on entirely different work than their parents. Women may take the same jobs as men. Child care can be shared. Gender roles have become fluid, allowing people of both sexes to express their individuality. A structure in which men and women have equal power, and in which children can comfortably talk back to parents (and rebel as adolescents), is the contemporary norm.

Yet modern societies have moved so far from patriarchy that immigrants from traditional societies can find the Western family incomprehensible. An antagonism to marital commitment would also be contrary to the values of a traditional society in which membership in a family determines identity. Some people in contemporary society no longer define who they are by membership in a group, but by a sense of personal uniqueness.

All these social changes have put marriage and family life under pressure. As extended family ties weaken, and communities lose social capital, nuclear families lack external support. The title of a book by Christopher Lasch (1977) nicely described the modern family as a "Haven in a Heartless World". Even the clergy have come to recognize the relationship between marital stability and social cohesion. At modern weddings, one hears less talk about maintaining religious faith and more about the need to root married life in a community.

Marriage and divorce

In modern society, in spite of (and in part because of) the ready availability of divorce, the quality of marriage has been going down (Amato et al., 2007; Cherlin, 2004). Paradoxically, this is happening because modern people believe that its main purpose is to create and maintain romantic bonds.

Passion, however exciting, lasts, at most for a few years (Fisher, 2004). If one accepts the idea that marriage has to be a lifelong romance, it is difficult to argue against divorce when people no longer feel "in love". One might believe in the possibility of a "no fault" divorce, if it were not for the fact children are so often involved. But the traditional idea that the main purpose of marriage is to raise children has declined (Whitehead, 1997; Wilson, 2002). And if parenting is not seen as the primary goal of family life, there are fewer reasons to stay together.

In modern society, few feel comfortable judging others for a decision to divorce. The response tends to be: "if that's what you need to be happy, I don't have a problem with it". Individualistic values allow for no other reaction. If the only purpose of living in a family is to meet personal needs for intimacy and romance, the right to dissolve a marriage is just another form of freedom.

An alternate way of looking at marriage is to view it as a task and a commitment. There is no such thing as unending bliss, and romantic feelings should not be expected to remain the same—even if love can be rekindled and transformed (Fisher, 2004). Living successfully with another person requires constant *work*.

Life experiences lead some to find marital life particularly disappointing. If one marries to escape one's parents, one may find family obligations equally oppressive. If one marries to seek out the affection one missed growing up, one quickly discovers that living in a couple is not a recipe for unconditional love. (It has been said that infancy is the only chance to be loved unconditionally, and even that is not possible.)

Ending a marriage to search for "true love" elsewhere is not usually a good option. In a famous quip, the English writer Samuel Johnson described a second marriage as "the triumph of hope over experience". Most divorced people do remarry, but second marriages are more likely than first marriages to be dissolved (White, 1990; Cherlin, 2004), and third marriages have an even higher rate of dissolution (Strow and Strow, 2006). (Multiple divorces affecting the same people inflate overall rates in the community, which are not therefore, as often claimed, as high as 50%, but closer to 30%.) Thus, while some people are happier the second time around, there are good arguments in favor of trying to work things out if that is possible. If you want too much from intimacy, you are bound to be frustrated. In this way, narcissistic traits often lie behind the instability of second marriages. If you have problems with commitment, and/or unrealistic expectations, marriage may not be different with a different partner.

Attitudes toward divorce reflect wider social forces that have undermined the value given to family life. I have treated young adults for most of my professional life and have heard many express disdain for marriage. Their contemptuous view of family life focuses on an image of the proverbial "white picket fence and 2.5 children". Marriage is seen as a trap and an illusion.

In some cases, earlier experiences (unhappily married parents or parental divorce associated with conflict and/or abandonment) shape these perceptions. But anti-family rhetoric is broadly prevalent in modern society. When peer groups support the well-known statement, "marriage is just a piece of paper", many will see it exactly that way. (But if a contract is only a piece of paper, why not sign it?) Hostility to the formality of marriage is based on the idea that commitments tie you down. When individual needs come first, social structures of all kinds can be seen as oppressive.

Anti-family rhetoric, which goes back to Engels in viewing the family as an obsolete bourgeois prejudice, misses most of what is crucial about marriage. The family is a social commitment, with the raising of children as its central purpose. That is why its structure remains basic for most of us. Most people end up either married or living in a long-term relationship. But since the traditional social stigma of remaining single has greatly declined, people have more options. Family life is most definitely *not* for everyone.

Living together

Marital breakdown has fewer practical consequences than it once had. Laws have changed to reflect this situation. Divorce and remarriage are relatively easy. And in a practical way, marriage is less necessary today. A woman can have her own job and raise a child without a man if she so chooses. More women are making these choices. Yet, while common-law marriages are more frequent, they are more unstable (National Marriage Project, 2000) and may not therefore be the ideal way to raise children.

Given the rate of divorce in the modern world, some are reluctant to marry at all—either the first time or on subsequent occasions. Common-law marriage has accordingly increased in popularity. It can be particularly attractive to those who were previously married. However else they rationalize it, most people see the dissolution of marriage as a personal failure. In this view, the break-up of a live-in relationship doesn't "count" in the same way.

Marriage was long supported by a culture in which people were taught to be ashamed if they had children outside of the nuclear family. That is no longer the case. In Québec, where I live, the Catholic Church once dominated the culture. Now religion meets with almost total rejection, and marriage rates have gone down precipitously. More people live alone, and a whole generation prefers to live together rather than marry (either in Church or through civil alternatives). Since so many ex-Catholics are now openly opposed to legal marriage, rates are lower in Québec than in the rest of Canada.

Some people think that living together before marriage is a good preparation for a permanent bond. That turns out *not* to be true. While research shows little effect from short periods of cohabitation, the longer people live together before marrying, the more likely they are to divorce (National Marriage Project, 2000; Waite and Gallagher, 2000; Dush et al., 2003). The reason is that a weakness of prior commitment ultimately destabilizes marriage. Cohabitation has become a frequent pattern prior to marriage, particularly as a short-term arrangement. Yet living together for many years without any formal commitment makes it more likely that relationships will end, and divorce is more common even if the couple eventually marries. Moreover, while the divorce rate is high, the chances of staying together if one never ties the knot and only cohabits are even worse (Cherlin et al., 1991). Hesitation to commit to a permanent relationship may not go away when the knot is tied.

In all jurisdictions, the law requires child support by parents after separation. Yet while the financial rights of a common-law spouse are not the same, society is tending to see common-law relationships in much the same way as marital unions. This is another way in which the sanctified status of marriage has suffered decline. The pattern of cohabitation has stimulated a new vocabulary, in which the words "partner" or "life partner" replace "husband" or "wife". The use of these terms, derived from business arrangements, underlines the idea that the arrangement is voluntary and need not be permanent. There is nothing sacred about a partnership—you can always dissolve it.

While most people still marry and have children, over the last several decades, marriage has been undertaken at an older age (Amett, 2000). One reason is because it now takes longer to launch a career. Actually, the current age at marriage (late 20s) corresponds to the average during most of history. The very early marriages that were so common after the Second World War were historically aberrant and may have been a reaction against conditions during the Great Depression, when fewer people had enough money to marry (Elder, 1974).

In summary, the family may be under siege, but it will not disappear. Human needs for attachment and procreation must be met somehow. No one has found a better way to meet the universal need for attachment, and no one ever will. The challenge for the modern family is to remain stable while allowing for greater individual freedom and incorporating new social principles such as female equality and protection for the rights of children. Marriage may not be error-proof, but is unlikely ever to become obsolete.

Narcissism and romantic love

Falling in love is easy. Living with another person is hard. Romantic love involves a process of idealization in which the other person is seen as a perfect match and a soul mate (Person, 2007). At that stage, lovers may feel "made for each other." In the madness of love, the image of the beloved is remade to conform to one's own needs. The lover is seen as a mirror of the self and differences are downplayed.

In this way, a degree of narcissism lies behind every intense romance. The belief that one has found the *ideal* lover is an illusion and an unstable basis for lasting intimacy. As the real characteristics of the beloved become apparent, and differences accumulate, a degree of disillusionment is inevitable. One can get past that stage, but not everyone does, which is one reason why relationships based on romantic love can be unstable (Fisher, 2004).

A patient once told me that she would be disappointed to agree with my view that falling in love depends more on inner readiness than on the qualities of the beloved. In that case, *any* reasonable person might do. Actually, that was exactly my point! My patient was troubled by the idea that the man she would love might not be an ideal soul mate. I did not think the absence of perfection to be a problem. (But I was not surprised that the marriage she did eventually embark on ended in divorce.)

Many books have been written about how romantic love develops, from novelists (Stendahl, 1822/1983) to psychoanalysts (Person, 2007). Research psychologists (Tennow, 1999; Sternberg, 1988), as well as anthropologists (Fisher, 2004), have examined the process of falling in love in detail. Less has been written about why love does not always last.

In his novel *Anna Karenina,* Tolstoy famously wrote, "Happy families are all alike; every unhappy family is unhappy in its own way."

In the past, many marriages were unhappy, but divorce was difficult to obtain (or prevented by religious proscriptions). But people have not always looked to marriage as a way of satisfying all their needs for intimacy. When a spouse is one's only friend, the relationship is at greater risk. This is why it is important to lower the pressure on marriage, by investing oneself in other relationships and other social roles.

Many social scientists have concluded that one of the main reasons for the current high rate of marital dissolution is that too much is expected from a single relationship (Turner, 2004). Traditional marital life provided more structure than rapture. People in traditional societies did not require spouses to be confidantes and best friends. A community was available to serve those functions. But in a socially fragmented world, lovers may want *everything* from an intimate relationship. In the words of a popular 1969 song by Waylon Jennings:

> We'll build a world of our own that no one else can share
> All our sorrows we'll leave far behind the stairs
> And I know you will find peace of mind
> And we'll live in a world of our own.

Nice lyrics—but what a disastrous recipe for intimacy! The song reflects a narcissistic view of the world, in which a couple expects to fulfill *all* of each other's needs, outside of any social context.

What actually happens when people try to live out such a fantasy? The most likely outcome is separation or divorce. A fantasy of perfection and fusion cannot survive long. Thus narcissism, even when it creates a mutual admiration society in the short term, makes it difficult to stay married.

I once described shared narcissism in marriage as a "deathly embrace" (Paris, 1991). I used this metaphor to refer to a psychological symbiosis in which partners see themselves as one person. But love eventually converts symbiosis into differentiation. If romance does not evolve into a loving partnership, relationships may last no more than a few months or years (Fisher, 2004).

Otto Kernberg (1995) has movingly described how people need to overcome narcissism to preserve love. If you cannot separate self from other, your relationship will be unstable. Once you realize that the other person has different needs and that partnership rather than fusion is required, you have taken the first step on the road to mature intimacy.

The dénouement of the search for "perfect" love was memorably described in Tolstoy's *Anna Karenina*. A married woman falls violently in love with a military officer. After conducting an affair, the couple leave Russia and live together in Italy. Cut off entirely from their own social milieu, they find the days weighing heavily on them. They become bored and irritable with each other and feel that life has little purpose. The lovers return home after a few months, and the story ends with the heroine's suicide. In an important sub-plot, Tolstoy contrasts this outcome with that of another couple who build a successful marriage on shared ideals, shared work, and the raising of children.

To maintain intimacy, it helps to have an adaptive personality. Research shows that high neuroticism and impulsivity are associated with marital dissolution (Kelly and Conley, 1987). But everything depends on how your personality fits in with that of the other person.

Some of the most fruitful current research derives from the direct examination of interactions between married couples. One of the most widely quoted studies was carried out by Gottman et al. (2002), who followed a group of couples for several years after a series of initial observations. Negative marital interactions at baseline, even over short periods of time, predicted divorce. Gottman identified "four horsemen"—contempt, criticism, defensiveness, and stonewalling in response to conflict—as particularly strong predictors of marital dissolution.

Gottman's "four horsemen" overlap with many of the features of narcissistic personality disorder. Narcissism leads spouses to attack those whom they have loved or to withdraw from them, usually on the grounds that their own needs are not being met. Actually, marriages are more likely to survive when each person develops an identity and a purpose of his/her own. The French writer Antoine de Saint-Exupéry (quoted in Person, 2007), put the matter beautifully: "Life has taught us that love does not consist in gazing at each other but in looking outward in the same direction."

The idealization of intimacy

People in traditional societies were surrounded by images of gods. Today we live amidst pictures of sex and romance. Modern culture idealizes one-on-one intimacy. The love affairs of celebrities, like those of the gods of old, sell books, movies, and television shows that feed cultural fantasies.

The idea that love makes the world go round has also had a strong influence on psychotherapy. Many patients go into treatment because they cannot find love. Therapy may be deemed successful if it ends when a single person finds a life partner. One reads in books of therapists who receive a slice of wedding cake as a reward for their labors.

Yet even in the most successful relationships, intimacy is only the beginning of a long story. Romantic love lasts for a few years, after which idealization fades (Fisher, 2004). Now the loved one is seen in the full light of reality. For a relationship to continue and flourish, it needs to turn into a loving partnership. Instead of an endless state of bliss, married life consists of working together for common goals. A home has to be established and maintained. The rearing of children requires sacrifice, commitment, and teamwork. The couple will have less time for each other, and even less for themselves. But they still need to help each other to carry out common tasks. And when both spouses have careers, each requires emotional support to deal with the vicissitudes of the outside world. Finally, and crucially, couples need social networks, either shared or unshared, which lie outside the boundaries of intimate relationships and meet needs that intimacy cannot.

This is family life—the unglamorous subject that takes up most people's energies over decades, but is not always portrayed sympathetically. Of course, neglect of the daily and the mundane is nothing new. For centuries, literature and theatre have preferred to tell stories about falling in love or dying, not about raising children or going out to dinner. Evidently family life is not exciting enough.

While parents provide care for the next generation, they should not expect love and gratitude, even in return for a major investment of time and resources. To be satisfied as a parent, it should be sufficient to see one's children grow up to be healthy and productive. If children thank you and honor you, you are lucky. But it may not be wise to count on that.

The same principle applies to marital intimacy. Even with the best intentions, most people find that living with another person does not meet all their emotional needs. Why should it? A spouse does not necessarily have to be a soul mate. With time, people work around the boundaries and limitations of their marriage, make use of what is available in the relationship, and find other forms of satisfaction through work and a broader social life.

Psychotherapy and divorce

Psychotherapists often see people seeking help for marital problems. A question that often arises is whether patients having conflict with their spouse should be encouraged (or discouraged) to remain in a marriage (Kramer, 1997). A related question concerns whether parents should be encouraged to stay together for the sake of their children.

In principle, therapists are supposed to be neutral about such matters. But they rarely are. I know of a much-married psychoanalyst, many of whose patients ended up divorced. In contrast, a long-married therapist (such as myself) might have a bias in favor of keeping families together.

Biases flourish when there are no clear objective answers to questions. However, there is objective evidence that the two-parent family remains the best option for raising children. This is the way people have lived for thousands of years. It may not always work, but it should not be given up lightly.

Marriage is associated with better mental health than divorce or separation (Robins and Regier, 1991; Williams et al., 1999; Baumeister and Leary, 1995). The most likely reason is that adult needs for attachment are best met in stable relationships. Married people even have more active sex lives than single people (Laumann et al., 1994). The problem concerns the direction of causality. Is marriage good for mental health, or are people with serious psychological problems less likely to get married or to stay married? Both could be true.

If no children are involved, one might assume there is no "victim" in divorce. But that view only considers the individual. An alternative perspective is that marriage is a moral commitment, and that the pledge to remain together "for better of for worse" should be taken seriously. Abandoning someone who has made sacrifices for you (and who may or may not fully recover from losing the relationship) is an ethical issue.

There are many reasons for divorce, some of which are reasonable. Even in traditional societies, in which divorce was not allowed, not all people with alcoholic, unfaithful, or violent partners continued to live with them (Shorter, 1977). But in modern societies, divorce can occur for more casual reasons. It can take on the quality of bringing back a defective purchase to the store for exchange. Too often, the only reason for ending a marriage is the belief that one might be happier with someone else. Yet as we have seen, leaving your spouse for a "better" one can be an illusion.

The way psychotherapists view marriage reflects implicit cultural values. Patients are encouraged to talk about themselves for months of years at a time, often focusing on failures or deficits in current intimate relationships. But therapists only hear one side of the story and easily fall into trap of agreeing with patients that they have chosen the wrong partners. Few check these perceptions by directly evaluating couples and families. I have had some big surprises when I have done so. I found that while I was given an accurate picture of another person's irrational responses, I was not told what the patient did to bring them on.

Moreover, *everyone* has some tendency to see problems in intimate relationships as the other person's fault. Psychologists call that a "fundamental attribution bias" (Jones and Harris, 1967). We tend to see other people's misbehavior as reflecting their character, while our own mistakes are excused as reflecting a situation. Even people who are normally empathic with others may lose perspective when their own needs are at stake.

That is how married people affirm their own needs and their own point of view, while devaluing the spouse's perceptions. In their mind, it is the other person who is failing, for no good reason, to consider entirely reasonable and legitimate demands. Both husband and wife may see the situation precisely in this way. (In an old joke, a marriage counselor listens to a husband and wife relating problems with one another and tells each one "you are right"—and when asked "isn't it impossible that both can be right?" answers "you are also right".)

Psychotherapists are not supposed to take sides, but they often do. And there are ways to take sides without quite admitting one has done so. For example, a therapist may be "nonjudgmental" in not challenging the patient's point of view on an intimate relationship—a procedure that implicitly communicates validation. Another way to take sides (without overtly doing so) is by relating current problems to past events. Thus, if patients complain of not having their needs met, psychotherapists can point out that much the same thing happened in childhood with a mother or a father. (It might make more sense to point out that an adult cannot expect a spouse to act in a self-sacrificing way, as a child might expect from a parent.) Too often, the implicit message is: "you put up with this before and you are still putting up with it, but you don't have to".

In all these ways, psychotherapy has an intrinsic tendency to favor divorce. The values of our culture say that everyone is entitled to romantic happiness. Therapists have to bend over backwards to counter that idea.

Divorce and children

Does divorce increase the risk for children to develop psychological symptoms? The answer depends on how you interpret the data. Some have seen the cup as half empty, documenting the long-term effects of being brought up in single-parent families (Wallerstein, 1989). Quite a bit of research supports that conclusion (McLanahan and Sandefur, 1994). Yet other researchers see the cup of divorce as half full, emphasizing the frequency of resilience in children (Hetherington et al., 1985).

What makes the outcome particularly complex is that the negative effects of divorce on children, even if statistically more likely, are not predictable. A majority of children who grow up in broken families become perfectly normal adults (Cherlin et al., 1991). Moreover, not all divorces are the same. The most negative effects occur when parents are constantly quarreling, and when there is a toxic environment associated with substance abuse and violence. In such cases, children will be relieved when a marriage ends (Rutter and Rutter, 1993).

Paradoxically, the most serious sequelae of divorce ensue when a marriage is amiable on the surface and when children are shocked at their parents' decision to divorce. In one of the largest studies of divorce ever conducted, Amato and Booth (1997) analyzed their data by separating the effects of parental conflict from those of divorce itself. They confirmed that in the 30% of divorces that occur in highly conflictual marriages, children benefited from having their parents separate. But in the other 70% of cases, children did *not* benefit—and were more likely to develop psychological symptoms.

Ironically, it is the "no-fault" divorce that does the *most* damage. The reason is that children usually want to have two parents and consider their own interests not served if one or both decide they must live apart because they are "no longer in love" with each other. For children, single-parent families are rarely a first choice. People who leave partners in such circumstances sometimes tell friends, "the children are fine". Yet, as Amato and Booth (1997, p. 238) concluded: "future generations would be well served if parents remained together until children are grown . . . Spending one third of one's life living in a marriage that is less than satisfactory in order to benefit children—children that parents elected to bring into the world—is not an unreasonable expectation".

This research is highly relevant to the conduct of psychotherapy. Should clinicians consider the best interest of children when a patient is also a parent? The individualistic bias of psychotherapy does not routinely consider the interest of spouses as a legitimate concern. The welfare of children, even if they are unseen actors in the drama of psychotherapy, should also be taken into account.

A family systems perspective

To understand what is happening in intimate relationships, and to go beyond the biased account of one person, therapists benefit from taking a family systems perspective (Beavers, 1979). By and large it is a good idea to meet the family of a patient as part of an initial evaluation. And even if the family is not directly assessed, just thinking about how interactions work can help astute clinicians to read between the lines of a story. Pointed questions establishing sequences of events can often uncover the manner in which a patient has mishandled a situation or provoked a hostile response. I find this easier to do because I have had formal training in family therapy, which gave me experience directly observing marital interactions.

Most patients are sensitive enough to provide a reasonable picture for a therapist of what the important people in their life are actually like. But people who are highly narcissistic are unable to provide an accurate report of their intimate relationships (Kernberg, 1976). A narcissist's images of other people are often cardboard and one-dimensional. The partner's role is seen mostly in terms of whether *their own needs* are met—as opposed to understanding that other people have needs and that a compromise always has to be worked out.

Yet the best way to balance the negative effects of psychotherapy on marriage is still for therapists to meet directly with families. Couple assessment can clarify relationship problems, and it can be useful to make seeing the family of a patient a routine part of evaluation prior to starting treatment (Glick, 1980). Therapists can correct misperceptions through direct observation. This can allow them to help their patients see that what feels like an unprovoked attack is actually a reaction to what *they* are doing.

A family perspective also helps to overcome the intrinsic bias of individual therapy, which is to validate a patient's perceptions. Seeing relationships as a system also implies that neither party is being blamed for the problems they have with each other. Instead, therapists can encourage patients to think about how the other person is feeling. The process of understanding that other people are separate, and have their own feelings, requires empathy, and has sometimes been called "mentalization" (Bateman and Fonagy, 2006).

Nathan Ackermann (1958), an American psychoanalyst who became a pioneer in family therapy, introduced many of these ideas over 50 years ago. Yet family assessment is not routinely applied today. Patients who seek individual therapy, as well as their disgruntled spouses, are not always willing to be seen as a couple. Similarly, when the problem is a troubled child, not every family will accept being treated in therapy (which could be seen as implying that the parents are at fault). Yet there is no reason why psychotherapists cannot interview couples and families as part of the initial assessment, offer individual psychotherapy, and then carry out follow-up assessments during the course of treatment.

How psychotherapists view parenting

Most psychotherapists devote attention to the relationship between patients and their family of origin. That is often what clients often want to talk about. But psychotherapies that explain current problems as a result of defects in upbringing have a tendency to create conflict or to estrange patients, at least temporarily, from their families. And there is a real danger of blaming families for problems that belong to patients. To counter this tendency, one needs to understand and accept the deficiencies that are inevitable in all relationships, including that of parent and child. As parents sometimes tell overly critical children, "you will understand when you have one of your own".

Most people also need to maintain ties with their parents—even when current needs are not met. Relationships with the family of origin often improve when patients feel better. When people are no longer suffering, they have less reason to blame others. Even the way we remember parents in the past is influenced by the quality of our current relationship. A positive relationship with parents also becomes a real plus when children are born, since that is when grandparents begin to play a role.

When psychotherapists blame parents for problems, they assume that there is a "right" way to raise children. All kinds of unhappiness or misbehavior have been attributed to bad parenting. A myth has been created in which children are seen as almost entirely molded by their parents and in which failures of parenting are the main cause of psychological symptoms later in life (Paris, 2000). That is not even a half-truth—at best it is a quarter-truth. It is a belief that has hurt many parents—as well as their children.

A child is not a blank slate. Up to recently, social scientists tended to ignore or minimize the role of temperament in development (Pinker, 2002). Recent research in behavior genetics has shown that heritable factors play a much greater role (and that parenting plays a less crucial role) in development than previously believed (Plomin et al., 2001; Harris, 1998). Understanding these issues can help us to be more tolerant. Even therapists can have trouble in raising children. My view is that everyone is entitled to *one* difficult child. (Temperament is a lottery.) But if you have more than one troubled child, you may have done something wrong.

Invisible patients

Every psychotherapy session has invisible protagonists. If a patient is married, what you do in therapy can have great impact on a spouse. If your patient has children, what happens in treatment can have an important impact on them.

Therapists who treat people living in families can be considered to have *invisible patients* to whom they are also responsible. This concern is never far from my mind. I always try to get a sense of how spouses are functioning. I also want to know how children are doing (school performance is the best marker), and whether a parent's emotional problems have any impact on their development. Therapists have an ethical obligation to protect invisible patients. Even for the individual patient, being appropriately concerned about the welfare of loved ones and children is a sign of mental health.

I spent two years of my training at a hospital where family therapy was a central focus of teaching. Several of the faculty made it a point to meet spouses of patients who were undertaking extended course of individual psychotherapy. They would explain their procedure and warn the spouse that there might be periods of upset that could affect the marriage. These interviews also gave the therapists who conducted them the opportunity to carry out a reality check of who the spouses were—as opposed to how they were seen by patients. This family-friendly procedure assumed that therapy should assess the marriage, and determine whether it was viable. Then treatment could try to avoid being a threat to its integrity. Too often that is *not* the case. People come into therapy for marital problems, and then, as Nathan Ackermann once quipped—"two analyses can lead to one divorce".

Traditional therapy takes the point of view of one individual and validates it. Therapists may also tell patients that they were mistreated or misunderstood when they were children, and that they no longer need to accept such treatment. But feeling entitled is not conducive to making the compromises that keep relationships working. Is it any wonder that psychotherapy so often leads to marital dissolution?

Divorce is common enough—with or without therapy. Perhaps if marriages were more satisfying, patients living in families would not be seeking treatment in the first place. However, that begs the question as to why people feel more dissatisfied with their marriages than they did in the past (Amato et al., 2007). If couples want to stay together, they must work hard on a daily basis (Gottman et al., 2002). Those who hope to remain passionately in love are best advised not to marry at all.

The 1940s and 1950s saw the development of a powerful movement for marital and family therapy (Goldenberg and Goldenberg, 1999). At first as an outgrowth of child psychiatry, its ideas rapidly spread to other disciplines. Today professionals trained in social work dominate the field of family therapy. Some of its early leaders had worked with children and were not satisfied with the model then popular, in which a child was seen in play therapy, while a social worker counseled the parents. Another reason for the growth of the movement derived from problems in individual therapy. Many therapists concluded that they could only deal with marital problems directly by seeing couples.

Family therapy is based on a value system that challenges some of the biases of modern society. Its trajectory favors finding a way for people to stay together. Of course, all therapists accept that some marriages are better off being dissolved. But the overt aim of working with families is to keep marriages intact and ensure that children have two parents. Family therapists apply a wide range of techniques (Doherty and Simmons, 1996). The classic method, which includes children in every session, is less often practiced than in the past, while marital therapy for the couple is more commonly offered.

Couples usually come to marital therapy because one of the partners (more often the wife) is dissatisfied. But to get both spouses into treatment, they must have retained enough good feelings about each other to want to work to improve their relationship. The first job of a therapist in that case is to focus intervention on the marital *system* and to avoid getting overly involved in each person's complaints about the other. The goal is to negotiate a compromise in which both sides get something. Rather like diplomacy, the process requires a great deal of skill.

A large body of research has been published on the efficacy of marital and family therapy (Dunn and Schwebel, 1995; Wood et al., 2005; Asen, 2002). By and large, these approaches are as effective as individual therapy. But family therapy has a different purpose. This kind of psychotherapy treats a system, not a person.

Intimacy: Inside and outside the family

Relationships are important whether people live in families or not. Many patients who come to psychotherapy are not married. Some are too young, others are reluctant to commit, others are recovering from failed relationships, and still others prefer to remain single. Yet the main topics in typical therapy sessions derive from problems of intimacy.

The same principles that underlie family therapy can be applied to relationship issues. As we have seen, most people have a tendency to externalize interpersonal problems. When they have a conflict with a spouse or a lover, they will tell their friends (or a therapist) in great detail how the other person misbehaved and mistreated them. The answer can be, "you are probably right, but let's also look at your contribution, because if we don't, you can have no control over the situation". To be helped, people have to take "ownership" of problems.

Some people will rarely or never acknowledge what they bring to interpersonal conflict. (These are narcissists who may not benefit from psychotherapy.) Others may have to be dragged kicking and screaming into ownership, but eventually get the point. A few people do the reverse and blame themselves too much. (Those are the *easy* patients.) Most people, once they calm down after a conflict, can see the problem from both sides.

People being people, one often hears the plaint, "why should I have to change if he/she doesn't". The best response is to focus on consequences. Nobody is happy in a situation of constant conflict. You need to remember the good times you have had with the other person. (Maybe they still happen, between the fights.) If you want to hold on to a relationship, you have to work on it, even if doing so can be hard slogging.

One can explain to people who are ready to fight at the least provocation that this strategy accomplishes nothing. Therapists may have to combat that old chestnut, "shouldn't I be allowed to express my feelings?" But there is a big difference between understanding one's own feelings and dumping them on someone else.

Patients with a short fuse need to learn how *not* to respond, even to a clear provocation. Strategies for emotion regulation are relevant (Linehan, 1993). When a feeling is too powerful, you need to neutralize it before you can manage it. This may mean learning to "count to ten", distracting yourself, or just taking a walk around the block—whatever works. People who are emotional and easily angered need to learn how to stand back from a situation and not to get lost in their feelings. They need to observe their own emotions and think more about what other people might be feeling. In current jargon, this requires a capacity for "mentalization" (Bateman and Fonagy, 2006).

For some people, emotional conflicts are dealt with by avoidance and punishing withdrawal. As observed by Gottman et al. (2002), that strategy can lead to a vicious cycle—either one in which one person pursues a partner who always pulls away or one in which both withdraw, freezing each other out. To explain these problems, a therapist must (again) focus on consequences. I may say: "Do you or don't you want to keep this relationship going? If you do, you have to swallow your pride and be the first one to reach out." Or, as I have sometimes told patients, "You have to water the plants."

The same problems play out in friendships and in relationships to extended family, and the same principles apply to managing them. To maintain a friendship, you have to be empathic and tolerant of other people's foibles. Adults need to suck out whatever poison remains in their relationships to aging parents (and to siblings).

The attentive reader will note that none of these suggestions is particularly technical or profound. My comments to patients are certainly commonsensical, but they differ from giving advice—that famously problematic procedure. Therapists are trained to be tactful and know when to push ahead and when to back off—at least with their patients.

Psychotherapy is not an abstruse art that can only be learned through years of study and sacrifice. Even when you know a lot, you need to use common sense. One can use tricks from the cognitive toolbox (like emotion regulation) or psychodynamic interventions (e.g., "given the fact that your mother left the family and never came back, is it any wonder that you are sensitive to rejection?"). But the crucial strategy is to combat externalization. When patients say that their problems are the fault of an unsympathetic spouse or lover, the therapist should not be readily convinced. We choose people for a reason, and we have to learn how to bring out the best (not the worst) in them.

To deal with problems in relationships, psychotherapy needs to help people respect other people's limitations, as well as their own. Talking about problems effectively requires a sense of ownership. While there is no rigid formula, therapists can use the alliance to find coping methods that do not provide perfection but offer a manageable compromise.

In this context, it is worth noting what therapy should *not* do. One need not confine oneself to listening to people talk about their week and murmuring supportively. Therapy needs to be future-oriented and practical. It should challenge the idea that lovers, spouses, and bosses are the real problem or that a sense of frustration is a sufficient reason to leave a relationship or a job. The overall principle is that psychotherapists teach people to deal with the world as it is, not as they want it to be.

Spouses and lovers can only be disappointed if they expect each other to make them "happy". Parents are also likely to be disappointed if they expect their children to make them happy. People are more likely to enjoy their families if they see other relatives, have friends, do outside work, and participate in a community. The best protection is not to allow any single relationship to carry too heavy an emotional burden. Intimacy and community meet different attachment needs, and most people require *both* forms of affiliation. For this reason, we need to develop a wide range of attachments outside the immediate family.

In summary, psychotherapy, heavily influenced by the individualism and narcissism of modernity, fails to take social context into account. In a quest for freedom, we forget that intimate relations are designed for support and partnership and that to maintain these relationships, we need to learn that the world does not revolve around us, that happiness will not be absolute, and that the best results come from reasonable accommodations. Living with other people can teach us how to compromise, and how to care.

9
Building Social Networks

Balancing intimacy and community

Social networks are links between people based on common interests rather than on kinship. These networks meet needs that nuclear and extended families do not and cannot. Involvement in a community provides social support, and is therefore protective of mental health, whether or not one lives in a family (Cacioppo and Patrick, 2008).

Social capital (Putnam, 2000) is a related concept. It describes how networks produce a reserve of meaningful linkages, creating a sense of belonging. Like financial investments, one can accumulate social capital, which then bears psychological "interest".

A key principle is that it is risky to invest all one's emotions in a single relationship. Expecting one person to provide perfect happiness is like putting all your money in one stock. If it goes under, so do you. A more prudent strategy is to manage your emotional portfolio by investing in many different things. Social networks also provide more neutral emotional ground for making connections than intense intimate relationships.

While intimacy, when successful, can provide a large bonus in quality of life, it is rarely sufficient, by itself, for happiness. Finding a stable relationship need not be the primary goal of talking therapy. Instead, patients should be encouraged to connect with a wider community, to build social networks, and to accumulate social capital.

Career and commitment

Work is a major source of satisfaction in life. Not everybody can have a "career" (in the sense of a business or professional life built on personal commitment and choice). But people can still feel proud of mastering skills and accomplishments at work. A long-term follow-up of working-class men (Vaillant, 2002) found that as they gained increased responsibility over time (and generativity in relation to younger employees), they became more mature and dealt better with aging. Conversely, people who fail to realize these goals, particularly those who fall into chronic unemployment, are not contented with life and do not have successful relationships (Lester, 1996).

These principles apply equally to men and women. We no longer live in a society where women define themselves primarily by a family role. In fact, empirical evidence shows that marital stability is enhanced when women work (Schoen et al., 2002)—although some women still prefer to stay at home until their children are in school. Having a job outside the home provides an alternate source of status and satisfaction. Also, the workplace is a social environment where women can feel meaningfully connected without necessarily being intimate. If they are not entirely dependent on a husband for emotional support, work can help to stabilize the marital relationship.

One hears criticism of workaholics who define themselves by a job. Yet commitment to a career is strongly associated with mental health (Kessler et al., 2005). It is hard to imagine being functional or symptom-free when, in the absence of any physical or mentally disability, one has no social role. To participate in society and attain a degree of status means having a place in the world and feeling part of a community.

I advise patients that to recover from symptoms, they need to either work, or to go to school to prepare for work. Mental health is not promoted by permanent disability payments or long-term welfare. Society allows people to choose these options, but those who do are unlikely to benefit from talking therapy.

I do not consider giving a high value to employment to be a personal bias. Unless one is raising a child full time, not working means having no social status and usually leads to social isolation. Most chronically unemployed people have a marginal life, and their social network can be confined to a shopping mall. Some patients tell me they cannot work until they feel better. But they are unlikely to feel better sitting at home with little to do. In a wonderful phrase from Alcoholics Anonymous, "you have to fake it before you make it".

The ability to work generally precedes the establishment of stable intimate relationships. Erikson (1950) suggested that young adults need to develop an identity before they can undertake intimacy. Although there has been little formal research on this developmental sequence, it is in accord with my experience. I often advise young adults to put off getting seriously involved with another person until they have a job or are back at school. People who have no identity of their own expect too much from their relationships, which are then less likely to be successful. Falling in love is not a social role.

Therapists see that many unemployed people and patients with severe mental illnesses may not be able to work. But most suffer from less disabling symptoms and are capable of finding employment. Even if they have problems holding on to a job, they do not have an illness that actually *prevents* them from working. Unfortunately our social system makes it easy to find alternatives to employment. The system of disability payments was developed for medical conditions such as physical injuries or infectious diseases. One can estimate how long it takes to recover from a broken shoulder, or from a bout of influenza. The system might also be useful when applied to recovery from a brief period of depression. But it is less obvious how to predict a capacity to return to work when problems are chronic. If payments become an entitlement that a therapist is expected to support, that is poison for psychotherapy.

To motivate patients, I try to emphasize the consequences of unemployment. "Are you really happy staring at four walls? Does being on welfare make you feel bad about yourself? Are you meeting any friends this way? You cannot be happy if you spend your days sitting at home watching TV (or nursing grievances). You cannot wait to work until you feel right."

Psychotherapists also see patients who find jobs but do not keep them for long. They consistently get into conflict with colleagues or employers. In dealing with such issues, therapists need not agree with a patient's view that the job situation is the problem. Working as a psychiatric consultant in a general hospital, I am regularly asked to assess employees who are on sick leave because of psychological symptoms. If I were to believe some patients, there is not a single reasonable supervisor or head nurse in the hospital.

These scenarios resemble problems with intimacy in that one believes that a problem has arisen because of another person, rather than oneself. Again, therapists face the universal tendency to externalize. Yet every conflict is two-sided, and to make meaningful changes, one needs to stop blaming others and take *ownership*. In the workplace, one can be assertive without being aggressive or alienating. If my patients have a difficult boss, I try to empathize with the problem. But who ever had a boss who wasn't difficult? (I haven't.) But that need not mean that the patient has no options to improve the situation.

Building social capital

Family units develop within larger social networks. Extended family, with links to grandparents, siblings, uncles, aunts, and cousins, takes an important place in most people's lives. These contacts are essential but occasionally stressful. But while nuclear families can sometimes be emotional hothouses, extended family allows for a sense of connection on more neutral ground. Also, with rare exceptions, we are better off reconciling with our family of origin and forgiving our relatives their trespasses.

But people also need to belong to something lying outside the family orbit. Putnam (2000) emphasizes the importance of community activities: attachments and commitments outside the family that accumulate social capital. These links, in turn, protect the family. Belonging to a community provides a different sense of purpose from what one can expect from spouses or children. It has been known for half a century that integrated communities and social networks are associated with mental health (Leighton et al., 1963). People who do not belong to any social group are at greater risk for developing all kinds of psychological symptoms—as well as physical symptoms (House et al., 1988).

Another element of mental health is friendship. Having few or no friends is negatively associated with mental health (House et al., 1988). Same-sex friendships play a different role in people's lives than romantic intimacy. Unfortunately, some people are not good at them. Worryingly, research shows that Americans have fewer friendships than they did 20 years ago (McPherson et al., 2006). And given the tendency of modern people to belong to fewer community groups and to commit to fewer activities, social capital as a whole may be decreasing.

By and large, women are better at friendship than men (Baumeiser and Sommer, 1997). They connect naturally through talking, particularly to same-sex friends. I am always worried when a woman tells me that she can only relate to men—that usually means that sex and flirtation are being mistaken for intimacy. Men have a different way of relating, connecting through shared activities such as sports or games (Bell, 1981).

I often see women who want the man in their life to be a best friend. But that raises expectations that are not easily met—asking men to be more like women. The sexes have different communication styles: men tend to be supportive and practical but do not always have the listening skills that a female friend provides (Tannen, 1990). Another difference between the sexes is that men are more concerned about status, while women tend to put attachment first (Buss and Malamuth, 1996). That is probably why men tend to feel "one-down" when admitting weakness and may not base their friendships on talking about feelings.

These issues are less problematic when people meet social needs in multiple ways, outside of a single intimate relationship. Thus, married people often have dinner with other couples. Like soldiers fighting in the same foxhole, parents raising children exchange experiences. These relationships are different from, but complementary to, same-sex friendships.

Community service is a traditional venue for networking that has gone into decline in recent decades (Putnam, 2000). Yet therapists can specifically encourage patients to become "joiners" in an area of interest. There are many options, ranging from courses to causes. In principle, there should be something for almost everyone.

Organized religion is another key element in social networks—at least for those who retain either a faith or an attachment to a religious community. For those who believe, a sense of connection with and love from God can mediate life's disappointments. Yet even if one is not a believer, religious groups provide an important sense of shared commitment and connection that is strongly correlated with mental health (Koenig, 2001).

It may seem simplistic to state that people need to bowl, play cards, or go to church. But such activities, along with commitments such as volunteer work or fund raising, help to protect the family and provide crucial connections for those who do not live in one. I always ask patients about these links and am often discouraged to learn that they are absent. In spite of my own secular way of life, I have been struck by the role of religious affiliation in stabilizing people who would otherwise be unstable.

Without social capital, intimate relationships can collapse under the weight of excessive expectations. When social connections are weak, intimacy lacks a necessary buffer. I see many patients who have been hurt in romantic relationships because they were overly dependent on the approval of a spouse or a lover. One way to be less dependent is to access broader networks that meet different needs.

The ability to care for other people, for causes outside oneself, and for a wider community, is also an antidote to self-absorption. We may even see the world in terms of responsibilities, rather than "rights" that so easily turn into entitlements (Etzioni, 1993). Even in an era of cultural narcissism, many remain idealistic and motivated to serve their community. In a troubled world, there is no lack of social causes.

Alternatives to intimacy

Accumulating social capital is particularly important for the large proportion of people in modern society who choose to remain single. In the past, failure to establish a family was considered a personal failure, especially for a woman. (Men who chose to remain bachelors were not seen in that way, even if some were unhappy and lonely.) Given the biological imperatives behind a woman's desire for children, that issue may never disappear. But it is much easier now than it was 50 years ago to raise a child alone, and society has come to validate that choice. Moreover, women have many more options today, and their careers provide them with the opportunity to live full lives. They do not have to choose between marriage and a nunnery. Research consistently shows that feminist values maximizing choice have been good for women's mental health (Ballou and Brown, 2002). And those who do not marry are no longer condemned to taking on a traditional "spinster" role, spending their life caring for an elderly mother or for a sibling (although these options also remain legitimate).

Being single can sometimes be lonely, but not everyone is better off married. Not every woman is happier living with a man, and not every woman wants the responsibility of children. Like men who remain confirmed bachelors, some feel that commitment restricts autonomy. These people are better off remaining single. Again, raising a family is not for everyone. You have to be prepared for the consequences, particularly when children come. No one should underestimate how difficult it is to be a parent. Surveys in the community show that child-bearing women between the age of 20 and 40 have the highest levels of psychological symptoms (Robins and Regier, 1991).

In later middle age, life gets better for most of us. For those who marry, there is a tendency to mellow with age and to experience decreased levels of conflict (Vaillant, 2002). And when children are grown, it is not necessarily true that middle-aged people must suffer from an "empty nest". That scenario only occurs when a marriage is unhappy, or when other satisfactions (such as a career) are out of reach. Research shows that most feel better seeing children having their own lives and look forward to being grandparents (Raup and Myers, 1989).

These trajectories do not apply to all single people in the same way. But there are other options, even if they are not "traditional". One can live comfortably outside a family by developing a strong social network. I became interested in this issue after conducting a research project (Paris and Zweig-Frank, 2001). We followed up a group of women who had suffered from borderline personality disorder in their 20s. This condition, which mainly afflicts younger women, is characterized by emotional instability, suicidality, and unstable relationships. But most of our cohort never committed suicide and eventually found ways to get a life, even if their choices did not always lie in the mainstream.

After 27 years, when the cohort had reached a mean age of 50, I contacted most of them. Very few were still in treatment. Their lives had stabilized and almost all were working. Less than 10% still suffered from significant symptoms. The main consequence of their past troubles was that only half were living with a partner and only half had ever had children. But the decision to live alone was usually the right one. Those who had no partner lived lives capitalizing on personal strong points, while avoiding problems they could not solve.

Of all tasks in life, achieving success in an intimate relationship has to be the most difficult. Not everyone is cut out for the challenge. The research impressed me with how unmarried women can feel validated by work and can benefit from the support of social networks. Quite a few had joined churches. Many talked of close friends. Some spoke movingly about relationships with pets.

While some single people yearn for attachment and struggle for connection and meaning (Cacioppo and Patrick, 2008), others feel liberated to find their own direction in life. Psychotherapists need to validate these choices. We see many patients with long histories of difficulty with intimacy. They have found that being too close to another person creates excessive conflict and painful dependency. With time, they may learn being alone is not that painful, while pleasure also comes from doing things by oneself. To make a single life comfortable, people need other satisfactions: a commitment to work, an active social network, and a community that provides a sense of belonging.

A good example is the traditional pathway in which single women become schoolteachers. Doing so can give them an opportunity to shape the younger generation—without the stress of having their own children. (Parents do not get extended summer vacations.) And if you have no children, you have more energy for a social life and/or involvement in the community.

Being single need not, of course, imply celibacy. Research shows that most single women under 40 are sexually active (Lindberg and Singh, 2008). Psychotherapists should take an open-minded attitude to relationships with the opposite sex that fall outside the boundaries of family life. Short-term sexual relationships, love affairs, or "friends with benefits" can all provide meaningful satisfactions and a sense of connection.

Moreover, not everyone likes to be with other people all the time. Those who are highly introverted may prefer to live alone and have less emotionally intense relationships. These choices should not be viewed as in any way pathological. A wide range of fulfilling activities can be carried out alone. The options range widely, from vigorous physical exercise to photography. Again, psychotherapists should acknowledge individual differences and avoid promoting alternatives to intimacy.

Thus far, I have focused on problems in heterosexual relationships. The best-designed survey (Laumann et al., 1994) found that about 1% of the American population has a consistent homosexual interest. (The higher figures that are often quoted—5%, or even 10%—are either based on biased samples, or include people who are predominantly heterosexual but can "go the other way".) A fair amount of research has been conducted on the homosexual population. One of the most consistent findings is that this population is more likely to seek psychological treatment (Cohler and Galantzer-Levy, 2000). Obviously, therapists, whatever their own orientation, need to understand the gay world.

Homosexuals have a statistically higher frequency of psychological symptoms (Cochran and Mays, 2000; King et al., 2003). The most frequent are substance abuse, depression, and suicide attempts (Remafedi, 1999). These problems could reflect the effects of discrimination, and no doubt stigma and homophobia play some role. But gay culture may not provide the same stable support as a family. Short-term attachments and "cruising" are common in this community (Symons, 1979; Diamant and McMulty, 1995). Even when homosexuals live together, they may not be monogamous (Cohler and Galantzer-Levy, 2000). Intimate relationships do not generally last as long as in heterosexuals (Kurdek, 1998).

Therapists who treat gay patients need to understand these dilemmas. Like heterosexuals facing similar issues, they can avoid over-investment in intimate relationships and find alternatives through work and social networks. A rewarding job and an accumulation of social capital helps to buffer these problems.

Love, work, and community

Sigmund Freud was right to conclude that love and work are the best signs of mental health. But he undervalued the importance of attachments that come through belonging to a larger community. Freud was an individualist and a true son of the modern age who thought there is an absolute and necessary conflict between individual needs and the demands of civilization (Freud, 1930/1989). Actually, what is good for communities can also be good for individuals. Love and family life rarely meet emotional needs fully. Moreover, the more affiliations people have elsewhere, the better protected are their intimate attachments. Even people in happily committed relationships still require a community.

Psychotherapists can put more emphasis on these issues. Talking therapy can help people to extend their social networks and build their social capital. For most of human history, people have been happiest when they had a sense of belonging. Modern life may have made belonging more difficult, but it is far from impossible.

10
Practicing Psychotherapy in a Social Context

This book is not a "how to" manual for psychotherapy. Talking therapy is a personal art, and perfectly good clinicians do things quite differently. Nonetheless, a few general principles follow from the themes developed in previous chapters.

Most important, psychotherapy is a social intervention conducted in a social context. It is surprising how little attention has been paid to this principle. Therapy is often written about as if it exists only in the minds of patients and therapists. That reflects our modern focus on individualism. This perspective makes inner exploration, whether of fantasies and memories (as in psychoanalysis) or of cognitive schemas (as in cognitive behavioral therapy (CBT) the main point of therapy.

My view is different. The best use of talking therapy is to help people *get a life*. That means actively promoting commitments in the real world. It means having a social role through work, as well as building social networks in the community. Focusing on the social context of psychotherapy also leads to a somewhat different set of procedures for the conduct of treatment.

Contracting and setting goals

Setting formal goals has become part and parcel of many activities that used to be left to chance and custom. Anyone who starts a company is expected to write a business plan. Educators are expected to set objectives and to ask their students whether they have been met.

In much the same way, therapy is a contractual arrangement. A service is being paid for (either directly by the consumer or through insurance) and the "deliverables" need to be spelled out and defined. Setting a time frame by which treatment should be concluded, and reviewing progress every few months, is part of that process. Some therapists use signed contracts and scheduled performance reviews as an integral part of treatment. With or without such formality, target symptoms and behaviors still need to be identified and kept in sight.

In the absence of a time frame and set goals, talking therapy has a distinct tendency to go nowhere. Yalom and Leszcz (2005) humorously called this scenario "cyclotherapy"—a process that goes around in circles. I often hear about this when I do consultations with people who have had unsuccessful courses of talking therapy. Patients tell me they went regularly to sessions and discussed current life problems. Their therapists listened sympathetically, but the treatment went nowhere. Without established goals, talking therapy drifts and sometimes becomes interminable.

If goals have never been defined, it is difficult to say whether treatment is or is not working. That is a particular problem for open-ended long-term therapy. Defined goals lead talking therapy to be focused and brief. Long-term therapy, with its broader aims of self-discovery and personality change, has no obvious endpoint. In contrast, brief therapy is a targeted approach whose aim is to get people back on their feet. Short-term treatment should be the default condition of talking therapy, with longer courses reserved for treatment-resistant cases. Even then, extended treatment should be prescribed with caution, since patients who do not benefit from a short course do not always do much better when treatment is open-ended (Kopta et al., 1994).

The doubtful reputation of talking therapy is almost entirely due to the prescription of open-ended therapies that go on for years. Treatment drifts, and talking becomes more of a personal quest than a treatment. Like religious and spiritual journeys of the past, it is a voyage into the unknown. As Joseph Campbell (1949) described in his book *The Hero with a Thousand Faces*, a quest is a quasi-mythological venture, which involves leaving home and safety, facing and overcoming dangers, and returning to where one started from (without ever being quite the same person again). For a famous fictional treatment of the theme, one might read *The Lord of the Rings* (Tolkien, 1991). A quest is not carried out alone but with crucial help from an expert guide. Like other spiritual journeys, it requires a sacrifice of social networks as energy is diverted to explore the inner world of the psyche.

A personal quest can take a toll on others. I sometimes hear complaints from the spouses of patients about the impact of living with someone who is self-absorbed in therapy for years. In spite of the best intentions of practitioners, open-ended therapy encourages self-involvement. An endless search for "insight" fails to teach realism, compromise, and maturity.

When patients come to therapy to relieve symptoms, treatment has a clear goal and can be terminated after a brief course. But if treatment is a quest to find oneself, or to attain happiness, it lacks a defined end point. That scenario is particularly associated with psychoanalysis and derives directly from the nature of its procedure. But the problem is not unique to any method. In its original form, CBT was associated with a time limit and specific goals, and clinical trials have examined its effectiveness over a period of months. Yet patients are not always satisfied with small victories. That is why some of my colleagues who practice CBT also go on seeing people for years—just like psychoanalysts.

Ironically, patients who are least likely to benefit from open-ended therapy—those with narcissistic traits—are particularly attracted to this kind of treatment, because it so effectively meets their need to be the center of attention. These are people who love to talk about themselves, and therapy provides them with an attentive listener. Yet doing so does not guarantee a benefit. In common parlance, people "talk the talk" but do not "walk the walk". It is all too easy to enjoy talking about problems without doing anything about them. This is why the aim of treatment should be practical—focusing not on insight into the psyche, but on "getting a life". And that is why therapy needs to establish a structure from the very beginning.

When therapy begins, one should already start thinking about how to end it. A time contract should be established: six months, or at most one year. If more time should turn out to be needed, another contract can be made. Or, one can plan breaks in therapy (with a return for "tune-ups"). Even if not all problems are resolved at the termination point, therapists should have confidence that patients can work on them independently. Patients who come only for a few months can still learn to apply what they learned in the consulting room to the real world.

This approach is in broad accord with the research literature. A classic study (Howard et al., 1986) found that half of all patients in therapy lose their initial symptoms within ten weeks and that two-thirds do so by 20 weeks. Thus, a course of 10–20 sessions is effective for most problems, while treating patients for longer periods runs into a law of diminishing returns (Kopta et al., 1994). Moreover, while the evidence for open-ended therapy is weak (to the point of being absent), support for brief courses of treatment is quite strong. This finding is independent of specific models and applies to short-term psychodynamic therapy (Crits-Christoph and Barber, 1991; Leichensring et al., 2004; Abbass et al., 2006), as well as to CBT (Beck, 1986). Moreover, patients (with the exception of those who specifically seek open-ended treatment) do not spend long periods in treatment: surveys show that psychotherapy in practice is usually brief (Gabbard et al., 1997).

Life is full of trouble and conflict. To be symptom-free or "completely analyzed" is an illusion. No matter how healthy your life style, you cannot prevent illness. Similarly, no matter how mentally healthy you think you are, you cannot live free of psychological problems. Time limits and specified goals focus patients on the art of the possible, not an impossible quest for a new self. Finally, ending a course of treatment need not close the door to further therapy. Sometimes people need a different type of treatment at different times, and at different stages, depending on their life circumstances.

A similar approach was first proposed over six decades ago. Franz Alexander and Thomas French (1946) were pioneer psychoanalysts who first proposed an "intermittent" model. Alexander and French observed that continuous treatment works against the goals of autonomy and mastery that psychotherapy aims to achieve. Instead of keeping patients in continuous treatment, they recommended asking them to try things on their own for a while. Patients could then return for another course later, if required. It is likely that therapy is often practiced intermittently, and research shows that people who obtain access to talking therapy do not restrict themselves to one course in a lifetime (Cummings and Sayama, 1995).

All these procedures assume that patients are coming to treatment to modify their behavior. That is not always the case. Some patients come for treatment but do not want to change. They are in what theorists on "motivational interviewing" have called a "pre-contemplation" stage (Prochaska et al., 1994), that is, they are only *considering* modifying behaviors. In such cases therapists can only explore the consequences of remaining in the same place, and formal treatment may not even be embarked upon but postponed. If patients are not ready to change, treatment can always be resumed at a later time when they *are* ready. Finally, psychotherapists need to accept the possibility of failure. If patients do not change within a reasonable time, there is no obligation to continue. As research shows, therapy does not always work. Without motivation, it is almost bound to fail. Clinicians should not try to do the impossible.

In the famous serenity prayer (originated by the theologian Reinhold Niebuhr and popularized by Alcoholics Anonymous), one asks "to accept the things I cannot change; courage to change the things I can; and wisdom to know the difference". The emphasis on acceptance and wisdom in these well-known lines applies as much to therapists as to patients.

A practical approach to talking therapy

To help patients get a life, therapy can encourage better management of interpersonal conflicts, a commitment to an occupation, and the building of social networks. That constitutes a clear agenda for change, and most patients will sign on to such goals. Some might ask whether it is right (or possible) for therapists to impose an agenda of any kind on patients. But no treatment has ever been conducted without a plan. The only question is whether the agenda is overt or covert. The art of talking therapy consists of knowing how to influence people without becoming domineering or insensitive.

Therapists have promoted the goals of work and love since the time of Freud. But the importance of social networks has not always been recognized. In every society and throughout history, people have lived in social groups and communities. Human beings are not made to be absolute individuals living in absolute freedom. Social commitments and networks are necessary for mental health.

Psychotherapy, a method designed to help people accommodate personal needs to a social milieu, has a role to play in restoring a balance between these forces. It arose to deal with distress in an era of alienation but became entangled with the very cultural narcissism that helped create it. Talking too much about the inner world runs the danger of becoming another vehicle for narcissistic self-regard and self-inflation. Therapy has to actively work *against* these values and promote a contrary point of view.

Traditionally, psychotherapy is supposed to be "non-judgmental". But no one can work on psychological problems without an explicit or an implicit set of values. The idea that therapists should never give advice reflects either a lack of experience or a rigid theoretical position. While advice must be offered sparingly, and while patients may not always be able to use it, it is an essential element of therapy.

Using therapy to combat narcissism

Taking social context into account can help individual patients. But the responsibility of psychotherapists goes beyond the person sitting in front of them. Consequences for other people, and for society at large, also need be considered. The millions of people who have been in psychotherapy give its practitioners a certain power. That power should be used responsibly.

Talking therapy emerged in an age of heightened individualism, and demand for this treatment has always been greatest in people on the vanguard of modernity. The "issues" that patients bring to therapists are also very modern. In a traditional society, few people would ask whether jobs or relationships are sufficiently "fulfilling" or whether commitments in life require too many compromises. In cultures in which self-realization is not valued, and in which family and community are more defining of identity than individual needs, most people accept their lot in life and "make do".

In contrast, some people in modern society believe in "self-realization" (Twenge, 2006). First described by Maslow (1943) as the highest level of a hierarchy of needs, this concept implies that people should, once their basic needs are met, expect to live out their lives in a way that corresponds to a sense of themselves as unique and special. It has become a powerful implicit value in many forms of psychotherapy. But while everyone needs to find a place in the world that makes them comfortable, few of us are that unique.

The very wish to be "in therapy" can be driven by personal and cultural narcissism. One can observe this in the way some patients talk about therapy experiences—idealizing therapists and describing an exciting journey to the heart of the psyche. Stories like this make me doubtful as to whether treatment is doing its job.

Narcissism makes people want to be perfect, have perfect partners, and have the best of everything life has to offer. They want to make good money, travel all over the world, eat exotic food, and send their children to the best schools. There is nothing wrong in principle with any of these goals. But the embrace of these values makes it more difficult to be satisfied with what life actually has to offer: average levels of success, financial constraints, and marital and romantic partners who are "good enough" but far from perfect.

Experienced therapists learn to counter these wishes and promote a more practical and connected approach to life. But to reach that point, they must confront their own narcissism. Therapists live in the same cultural world as their patients. Mature clinicians must learn to be satisfied with limited results and count them as a success. This is a mental set that leads to realistic goals, avoiding a "mission impossible".

Most of the patients therapists see can accept constructive criticism. If one is reasonably tactful, patients will understand that they misperceive interpersonal encounters and that they can handle their relationships better. But patients who are highly narcissistic resist this perspective. How do you convince someone to have realistic goals if they are grandiose and are prone to "crash" when their illusions are punctured? How do you convince someone who lacks the ability to empathize with others to less entitled and more considerate?

That is how narcissism interferes with the process of therapy. The wish to be validated (and admired) takes precedence over self-criticism. Clarifications or confrontations are seen as attacks, and the response can be angry or dismissive. I cannot say how many times patients with these problems have responded to the mildest criticism with narcissistic rage. Thus, when narcissism is "malignant", psychotherapy may not even be possible. The best one can do is to gracefully accept defeat. Fortunately, not all cases are so difficult.

While therapists work with patients to help them tame personal narcissism, talking therapy is conducted within a wider climate of cultural narcissism. These problems lie beyond the scope of clinical work. Some psychologists have suggested ways of raising children that counter narcissism and *instil* more traditional values (Twenge and Campbell, 2009). Although I am personally sympathetic to these ideas, we are a long way from evidence-based parenting.

Even so, an understanding of cultural narcissism is needed in the clinical encounter. One of its most important implications concerns the benefits and limitations of close relationships. Research suggests that people in modern society have unreasonable expectations of intimacy (Prager, 1997). Love, no matter how passionate, is not enough for stability. Since not every need can be met in intimacy, relationships may be more stable when people have friends, extended family, and a community. Conversely, the weakness of ties to extended family and community in modern life adds greatly to the instability of intimate attachments. When love is everything, it ends up being nothing.

Similar principles apply to the modern preoccupation with sexual satisfaction. Sex, in the absence of a commitment to another person, cannot answer basic human needs for attachment. Twenge (2006) notes that in spite of "free love" and the ready availability of "hookups", young people today are even lonelier than they were 20 years ago.

Understanding the limitations of love and sex is essential for helping people to navigate modernity. Mental health is easier to achieve if we spread ourselves around. Like a balanced investment portfolio, our lives are just a little safer if we have more than one thing—a job, a lover, a family, friends, and a community. Problems in intimacy are more manageable when people also have community ties and meaningful commitments. Patients may not walk out of therapy feeling happy. But they can be more committed and more connected.

How therapy can build social capital

I am an old-fashioned psychiatrist, in that I still conduct psychotherapy. That is because I specialize in borderline personality disorder (BPD), a condition for which talking therapy has the strongest research support (Paris, 2008b). While I am hesitant, without support from systematic research, to generalize from my clinical experiences, some of them illustrate points made in this book.

For many years, I worked as a psychiatrist in a university health service. Although most patients had serious problems, treatment was made easier by the fact that they were in school. Some of the young adults I saw had a surprising ability to succeed academically in spite of mental disorders as serious as psychosis. Moreover, they had many opportunities to connect with a community created by a large university. One patient I treated with a severe personality disorder, and who made multiple suicide attempts, found a sense of connection through political activism, becoming the editor of the campus newspaper.

I prefer to work with sicker patients because I want to be sure that my efforts actually make a difference. I have always been particularly interested in patients who are chronically suicidal, most of whom have a diagnosis of BPD. Later in my career, I became a researcher on this condition. In the last ten years, I have developed specialized clinics to provide patients with optimal treatment. Specifically designed methods of talking therapy are the most evidence-based form of treatment for this population (Paris, 2008b). Although some of these patients do eventually commit suicide, the vast majority do not, in spite of having threatened to do so for long periods. These are people who need to keep their exit options open, so that being suicidal actually helps them to stay alive (Paris, 2006). I have stopped worrying about them, and now focus my efforts on helping patients to find a place in the world.

Recently, I have been working with a more disabled group of BPD patients who come to hospital clinics. These are cases in which rehabilitation presents a greater challenge. Not only are relationships highly disturbed, but these patients are often unemployed, and have little social capital to treat this population, it is an advantage to have multidisciplinary teams, including clinical psychologists, nurses, and social workers. Working in a team sharing a common vision provides support and consultation for therapists who are dealing with difficult patients. My experience in working in a specialized personality disorder clinic has also made me wonder about the model of solo practice that is generally used to provide psychotherapy. Even with less severely affected clients, working alone has limitations. Many patients in office practice might gain greater benefit if they had access to a wider range of services.

A more general implication of this work, discussed in the previous chapter, is that identity in young adults must be developed before intimacy can be successful. That is an old principle (Erikson, 1950), but the belief that love conquers all makes us forget it. Many of our patients are emerging from broken relationships. Our team advises them to "take a break" and make a better life plan before investing, or over-investing, in one person. Work may not always be a prelude to love, but love without work puts too much pressure on intimacy. We also help patients to develop social networks (friends, extended family, community) to buffer problematic intimacy. Those who are unemployed are encouraged to either seek employment or to go back to school to get the skills they need to be employed. We tell patients that they cannot better unless they do so.

Our program, designed for a dysfunctional group of young adults, has not been subjected to clinical trials, but it is consistent with the empirical literature, and we have carried out pre-post comparisons to document that treatment keeps these patients out of the emergency room—mainly by reducing the frequency of overdoses and self-harm. I can illustrate success in this population by describing patients who returned to the work force, as well as patients who accumulated social capital in other ways. One woman had a turning point when, after several years on welfare, she took training to be an airline stewardess. This was a big step for this patient, who had never previously been on an airplane. A responsible job made her feel that she had a role in the world, and it also provided a community of co-workers to which she could belong. She no longer felt, as she had in the past, that her life had no meaning without an intense attachment to a man. Another patient, a university student who had long-term problems with men, found meaning by founding a charity. She raised money to build a school in a developing country and spent every summer supervising this work. She also found a sense of community with the group of volunteers she recruited to run the fund-raising effort.

The task of treatment can be viewed as an opportunity to review a patient's psychological investment portfolio. Or to apply another metaphor, psychotherapy guides them from a hothouse of intense intimacy to the cooler ground of social roles and networks. It has often been said that it takes a village to raise a child. But the need for attachment to a wider society continues to be important throughout the life span. In spite of all the pitfalls I have discussed, therapy, when successful, does raise self-esteem. But an empty self cannot be so easily filled. People cannot have an identity without a community.

11
The Future of Psychotherapy

Talking therapy faces a crisis that threatens its future. Overshadowed by drug treatment, its prestige has greatly declined. Psychological therapies are not always carried out with expertise, and high-quality treatment is not consistently accessible. Finally, psychotherapy can work against its own goals.

The declining prestige of psychotherapy

While more people have access to mental health care, the leading edge of treatment today is not talking, but prescribing (Mojtabai, 2007, 2008). Impressive advances in neuroscience have created a zeitgeist in which treatment consists of correcting a "chemical imbalance". Many believe that all people need to get over anxiety or depression is the right medication cocktail. Physicians who prescribe drugs for psychological distress may not even take the time needed to find out what is troubling patients (Paris, 2008a; Carlat, 2010).

Yet many of the reasons for the declining influence of psychotherapy arise from its own failures. In the past, psychoanalysis was considered a "Rolls-Royce" treatment. While that conclusion was greatly mistaken, as long as people believed it, talking therapies had clout (Paris, 2005). Insurance companies sometimes covered extensive courses of treatment. But psychoanalytic therapy, which was sometimes endless, never proved itself empirically as either effective or cost-effective. As disillusionment with results set in, the zeitgeist changed.

Yet even today, most people, if asked to describe what talking therapy is, think of psychoanalysis and its variants. New Yorker cartoons still feature bearded analysts sitting behind couches. A generation ago, I knew a large number of people who were either "in therapy", who had been at some time, or who had a family member receiving it. The therapy culture was both influential and pervasive (Gross, 1978).

Few today hold these beliefs. Psychoanalysis is rarely sought or prescribed. Moreover, disappointment with the Freudian approach has affected the perception of all therapies. A pervasive *skepticism* has made talking about problems seem like self-indulgence. (And if psychological treatment is not conducted properly, that perception can sometimes be justified.)

Another reason for a decline in the prestige of psychotherapy is ideological and philosophical. It has long been an article of faith that applying reason to control the mind is a key to being mentally healthy (Ellis, 2001). That is what Freud hoped for, and cognitive behavioral therapy (CBT) holds much the same belief (Beck, 1986). Moreover, this point of view focuses on how patients cure themselves. In contrast, current views of mental illness do not expect people to actively combat their problems. Instead, patients put themselves in the hands of physicians who correct their faulty neurotransmitters. There are techniques for talking, but few things are as technological as a drug.

I am a psychiatrist who trained several decades ago, and I received a comprehensive training in the methods of talking therapy. Yet today, few of my colleagues practice formal psychotherapy for more than a few hours a week. Following breakthroughs in the treatment of severe mental illness, as well as significant progress in brain research, the field underwent a sea change, aiming to become just another specialty of medicine (Paris, 2008a). Psychiatrists no longer spend time collecting the detailed life histories that used to define their field. Evaluations are oriented to making diagnoses that meet criteria as defined by the *Diagnostic and Statistical Manual of Mental Disorders* (DSM), and symptoms are identified so that they can be targeted with drugs. Only a few training programs in psychiatry still devote time to teaching psychotherapy (Luhrmann, 2000). You do not even have to obtain access to a psychiatrist to receive prescriptions for drugs, most of which are being provided by family doctors and internists.

Neuroscience has taken on the glamour once attached to talking therapies. Everyone has seen the dramatic pictures created by brain imaging methods. (Not everyone knows that the colors are artificial.) It is tempting to believe that a deeper understanding of neurobiology will allow us to heal the mind. People who would have once sought out psychotherapy are now asking for (and receiving) drugs. And when these agents do not help, prescribing physicians prefer to search for the right cocktail and may not even consider referring patients for psychotherapy (Moncrieff, 2008).

While clinical psychologists remain much more interested in psychotherapy than psychiatrists, their niche is also under threat. Economic imperatives have also restricted access to services. The result is that only a minority of those who might benefit from treatment end up receiving it. And why would patients choose to go into psychotherapy if they believe that drugs can manage their symptoms faster and better?

I used to see many patients in consultation who expressed a wish to understand the unconscious processes and childhood experiences that would explain why their lives were so troubled. They had heard from the media (or from their friends) that the roots of life's sorrows lie in early experiences. Primed by these beliefs, they presented me with stories that would delight the heart of a psychoanalyst. They talked of domineering fathers and insensitive mothers. They believed that exploring how these experiences affected them would cure their problems. They were eager to talk about their past—even when their present life was a shambles. Today, patients seeking talking therapy are more likely to ask for a treatment that raises self-esteem or trains them to be less anxious. They conceive of therapy as a way of learning new skills and ask for CBT.

But other patients (actually most of those I now see in consultation) have little interest in talking. They believe in chemical imbalances, want their brains repaired, and ask for pills. These attitudes have spread to all social classes. One woman, who used to hold a responsible job, but who had been on welfare for years, blandly informed me that all she needed was a little more serotonin. (She believed that her current program for self-help – which mainly involved going to suntan parlors – was already raising her brain levels, but that antidepressants might be a useful supplement.)

In summary, the perception that drugs are more effective than talking has badly hurt the field of therapy. As psychiatrists have moved away from formal psychotherapy (Mojtabai and Olfson, 2008), psychologists and social workers became the main providers of this service. Unfortunately non-medical therapists are not sufficiently supported by insurance to fill the gap. Sometimes you can find a psychologist who works for a hospital (or for the National Health Service in the UK). But most of the time, if you want psychotherapy, you have to work hard to find it.

The quality of psychotherapy

Psychological treatment remains more an art than a science. Only a minority of therapists have been trained in evidence-based methods (Weissman et al., 2006). Psychotherapy often consists of little more than a supportive contact with a sympathetic listener. While most methods work in more or less the same way, every treatment needs a plan. Moreover, some patients (those with substance abuse, personality disorder, or psychosis) need specific and structured approaches that require special training.

Talking therapy should be supported by research, and practice should be evidence-based. The field will die if it fails to be firmly based on empirical data. The modern world gives great value to the scientific method—and rightly so. Rational treatment for medical or psychological symptoms always requires systematic investigation. But while talking therapy has received a fair amount of support from research, clinical practice can be dispiritingly unscientific. Up to now, psychotherapy has been fragmented into a number of competing methods, few of which are based on science. Talking therapy has promised too much and delivered too little.

Most patients improve with focused and time-limited methods. Unfortunately, it is not widely known (either among therapists or among consumers) that brief courses of well-planned therapy can be highly effective, even for problems that initially seem complex. One of the main points of this book is that talking therapy should not become an end in itself. I have seen too many patients who become addicted to the process. If they can afford it, or if the treatment is fully insured, they continue with no end in site. This problem cannot be understood only in terms of self-indulgent patients or grandiose therapists. Endless therapy develops in a social context that supports endless introspection.

The modern world is what made talking therapy necessary. And it continues to shape the way the field has developed. Everyone needs a place to go when life is painful. The need for attachment and meaning is universal. But traditional methods of healing no longer work. When people have to find their own way in life, it is more difficult to meet needs for connection.

Ironically, these are the very problems that psychotherapy was invented to address. Yet talking to a therapist cannot fill needs that used to be met by society as a whole. If asked to do things it cannot do, talking therapy will face a crisis of credibility. As cultural narcissism permeated our society, some forms of psychotherapy promoted themselves as voyages of self-discovery. But "being in therapy" does not even begin to address the problems of living in the real world.

Understanding psychotherapy's crisis

I was trained to encourage people to stop blaming others and to focus on themselves. The same principle should be applied to the crisis facing psychotherapy. Instead of criticizing insurance companies or governments, practitioners should look at themselves and see how they could do better.

While this book has described the many problems facing talking therapy, it may be due for a comeback. Focused, practical, and evidence-based approaches are already reviving interest. People seeking help for psychological problems may not be aware that talking therapy is as evidence-based as any drug. If conducted properly, it can be a powerful tool for managing a broad range of psychological symptoms. While the largest body of evidence supports its use in common mental disorders such as anxiety and depression, it is now well established that specialized forms of therapy are helpful for patients with conditions ranging from personality disorders to psychosis. This method of treating troubled people needs better promotion.

The current fad for taking drugs for any and every psychological problem is bound to fade with time. Whenever a treatment is over-hyped, one can eventually expect a backlash. That may happen even faster than we think. The limits of antidepressants as a "cure-all" for problems in mood are now well established and widely known (Kirsch et al., 2008). Like talking therapies, drugs have promised too much and delivered too little. The current belief that they can manage almost any psychological problem is based on "hype", not science. This is not to say that drugs are any less than essential for the treatment of severe mental disorders. But these agents do not work for everyone, and sometimes they do not work at all. By and large, drugs are not consistently helpful for patients with common, less disabling symptoms (Moncrieff, 2008).

A swing of the pendulum back to psychotherapy might follow from disillusionment about currently overblown claims for drugs. There are many clinical conditions in which psychotherapy can be superior. Many patients currently being treated with drugs should be referred for this treatment (Moncrieff, 2008). These facts, once disseminated, could help talking therapy regain some of its former prestige—and become better insured. But psychotherapists also have a responsibility to change the current situation. They can raise the image of their profession by offering briefer, more targeted, and less expensive methods based on scientific evidence.

At the same time, psychotherapy needs to become more available and better regulated for quality. If patients could afford psychological treatment and find a competent therapist, fewer would end up on a treadmill of "medication adjustments". The irony is that just when we have enough evidence to show that talking therapy is effective, it has been overshadowed by less effective alternatives. Eventually people will realize they need better options. European countries, particularly the National Health Service in the United Kingdom, have been integrating more psychologists into the health system. These developments could cross the Atlantic and provide better access to therapy in North America.

The main obstacle to access is expense. Talking takes time, and time is money. But while psychotherapy can be expensive, so is a cardiac bypass (a procedure that is often fully insured, in spite of shaky scientific support). Talking therapy, even when conducted briefly, does cost more than a prescription. But insurers (and the public) need to understand that talking can still be the most cost-effective option. Psychotherapy actually saves money, by keeping patients from burdening the health care system (and by helping them get back to productive work). To give it a rightful place in the treatment of psychological symptoms, it should be insured for at least 20 weekly sessions per year.

Public confidence will only be earned by producing the same level of data for efficacy that would be expected for a drug and by practicing on that basis. Scientific data can be used to convince insurance companies and governments to provide better coverage. Practitioners have a role to play by spreading the word about the efficacy of psychotherapy.

At the same time, consumers have to actively lobby for better insurance coverage. Up to now, organizations such as the National Alliance on Mental Illness (NAMI) in the United States have concentrated on treatment for severe mental disorders and have been more interested in the price of drugs than in access to psychotherapy. They need to speak up for patients who are significantly distressed but not severely disabled.

To make the field of psychotherapy legitimate, it also needs to speak with one voice. That would be more likely to happen if it were a profession in its own right. While PhDs continue to be offered in clinical psychology, few programs provide a systematic clinical training. Moreover, graduates who devote their professional lives to treating patients need to belong to an organization that supports this kind of work. Instead of broader professional bodies (e.g., the American Psychological Association or the American Psychiatric Association), or associations supporting a specific technique (e.g., psychoanalysis or CBT), we need an organization supporting a single, evidence-based model of psychotherapy.

With the current Babel of therapy options, this is not happening. Each school of therapy concentrates on promoting its own model and its own methods, even as the public is being denied the benefits of treatment. Consumers may not want to accept this situation, but they need professional guidance to navigate choices. An accepted generic model based on general principles could then be tailored, rather than being marketed on "a one size fits all" basis (Beitman et al., 1989).

Talking about ourselves

The revival of psychotherapy can be aided by setting different goals. Talking therapy has to redefine itself as a practical method, not as an extended and interminable journey into the self but as an outward-looking procedure. It needs to address the real world, in which love is not perfect and jobs are not ideal. Patients need to emerge from talking therapy, not with higher self-esteem, but better equipped to get a life.

The modern world is here to stay. Short of some universal catastrophe, we can never return to a world of tradition and unquestioning belief. We must learn to live with a diversity of values. Many continue to need professionals to help manage their psychological problems. Yet periods of rapid change are often followed by periods of consolidation. The constraints of human nature suggest that a better balance between the individual and the social group is both necessary and possible. Cultural narcissism may already have peaked, as suggested by the reassuring fact that psychological symptoms (such as substance abuse and suicidality) which have been canaries in the mine are becoming less common. Perhaps society is entering a new phase, in which social commitments will be valued to the same extent as entitlements.

As the field matures, practice will change. Trendy and bizarre methods will die out. Future methods of therapy will be both practical and relatively brief. They will become accepted procedures that can be standardized and made readily available. Psychotherapy has given millions of people a valuable opportunity to talk *about* themselves. It need not encourage people to talk *to* themselves.

References

Abbass, AA, Hancock, JT, Henderson, J, Kisely, S (2006): Short-term psychodynamic psychotherapies for common mental disorders. *Cochrane Database of Systematic Reviews* 4 Art. No.: CD004687. DOI: 10.1002/14651858.CD004687.pub3.

Ackerman, NW (1958): *The Psychodynamics of Family Life*. New York: Basic Books.

Adams, F (1939): *The Genuine Works of Hippocrates*. Baltimore: Williams & Wilkins.

Alexander, F, French, T (1946): *Psychoanalytic Therapy*. New York: Ronald.

Amato, PR, Booth, A (1997): *A Generation at Risk: Growing Up in an Era of Family Upheaval*. Cambridge MA: Harvard University Press.

Amato, PR, Booth, A, Johnson, DR, Rogers, SJ (2007): *Alone Together*. Cambridge, MA: Harvard University Press.

American Psychiatric Association (2000): *Diagnostic and Statistical Manual of Mental-Disorders, 4th edition, Text Revision*. Washington, DC: American Psychiatric Press.

American Religious Identification Survey (2009): http://www.americanreligionsurvey-aris.org/, accessed March 15, 2009.

Aronson, E (1969): The theory of cognitive dissonance: a current perspective. In L Berkowitz (Ed.). *Advances in Experimental Social Psychology*, 4, pp. 1–34. New York: Academic Press.

Asen, E (2002): Outcome research in family therapy. *Advances in Psychiatric Treatment* 8: 230–238.

Auden, WH (1939/1979): In memory of Sigmund Freud, In E Mendelsohn (Ed.). *Selected Poems of WH Auden*. New York: Random House.

Back, MD, Schmulke, SC, Egloff, B (2010): Why are narcissists so charming at first sight? Decoding the narcissism-popularity link at zero acquaintance. *Journal of Personality and Social Psychology* 98: 132–145.

Ballou, M, Brown, LS (2002): *Rethinking Mental Health and Disorder. Feminist Perspectives*. New York: Guilford.

Barkow, J, Cosmides, L, Tooby, J (1992): *The Adapted Mind: Evolutionary Psychology and the Generation of Culture*. NY: Oxford University Press.

Baron, J (2000): *Thinking and Deciding*. Cambridge, UK: Cambridge University Press.

Bass, E, Davis, L (1988): *The Courage to Heal*. New York: Harper and Row.

Bateman, A, Fonagy, P (2006): *Mentalization Based Treatment: A Practical Guide*. New York: John Wiley.

Baudry, L (1986): *The Frenzy of Renown: Fame and Its History*. New York: Vintage.

Baumeister, RF, Leary, MR (1995): The need to belong: desire for interpersonal attachments as a fundamental human motivation. *Psychological Bulletin* 117: 497–529.

Baumeister, RF, Smart, L, Boden, JM (1996): Relation of threatened egotism to violence and aggression: The dark side of high self-esteem. *Psychological Review* 103: 5–33.

Baumeister, RF, Sommer, KL (1997): What do men want? Gender differences and two spheres of belongingness: comment on Cross and Madson. *Psychological Bulletin* 122: 38–44.

Beard, R, Berlowitz, L (1993): *Greenwich Village: Culture and Counterculture.* Rutgers University Press Piscataway, NJ.

Beavers, WR (1979): *Psychotherapy and Growth: A Family Systems Perspective.* London: Blackwell.

Beck, AT (1986): *Cognitive Therapy and the Emotional Disorders.* New York: Basic.

Beck, AT, Freeman, A (2002): *Cognitive Therapy of Personality Disorders,* 2nd edition. New York: Guilford.

Beitman, BD, Goldfried, MR, Norcross, JC (1989): The movement toward integrating the psychotherapies: An overview. *American Journal of Psychiatry* 146: 138–147.

Bellah, RN, Madsen, R, Sullivan, WM, Swidler, A, Tipton, SM (1985): *Habits of the Heart.* Berkeley: University of California Press.

Belsky, J, Vandell DL, Burchinal M, Clarke-Stewart KA, McCartney K, Owen, M (2007): Are there long-term effects of early child care? *Child Development* 78: 681–701.

Berman, M (1982): *All That Is Solid Melts into Air: The Experience of Modernity.* New York: Simon and Schuster.

Berne, E (1964): *Games People Play—The Basic Hand Book of Transactional Analysis.* New York: Ballantine Books.

Berrios, G, Porter, R (1995): *A History of Clinical Psychiatry: The Origin and History of Psychiatric Disorders.* London: The Athlone Press.

Beutler, LE, Malik, M, Alimohamed, S, Harwood, M, Talchi, H, Noble, S, Wong, E (2003): Therapist variables, In MJ Lambert (Ed.), *Bergin and Garfield's Handbook of Psychotherapy and Behavior Change.* New York: Wiley, pp. 227–230.

Bhar, SS, Thombs, BD, Pignotti, M, Bassel, M, Jewett, L, Coyne, J, Beck, AT: (2010): Is longer-term psychodynamic psychotherapy more effective than shorter-term therapies? Review and critique of the evidence. *Psychotherapy and Psychosomatics* 79: 208–216.

Biddle, L, Brock, A, Brookes, ST, Gunnell, D (2008): Suicide rates in young men in England and Wales in the 21st century: time trend study. *BMJ* 336: 539–542.

Bisson, JI, Ehlers, A, Matthews, R, Pilling, S, Richards, D, Turner, S (2007): Psychological treatments for chronic post-traumatic stress disorder: systematic review and meta-analysis. *British Journal of Psychiatry* 190: 97–104.

Bjorklund, DF (2000): *False-Memory Creation in Children and Adults.* Mahwah, NJ: Lawrence Erlbaum.

Bland, RC, Dyck, RJ, Newman, SC, Orn, H (1998): Attempted suicide in Edmonton, In AA Leenaars, S Wenckstern, I Sakinofsky, RJ Dyck, MJ Kral, RC Bland (Eds), *Suicide in Canada.* Toronto: University of Toronto Press, pp. 136–150.

Borch-Jacobsen, M (2009): *Making Minds and Madness: From Hysteria to Depression.* Cambridge, UK: Cambridge University Press.

Bowlby, J (1969, 1973, 1980): *Attachment and Loss,* 3 volumes. London: Hogarth Press.

Branden, N. (1969): *The Psychology of Self-esteem.* New York: Bantam.

Brown, DE. (1991): *Human Universals.* New York: McGraw-Hill.

Buckley, P, Karasu, TB, Charles, E (1981): Psychotherapists view their personal therapy. *Psychotherapy* 18: 299–305.
Buss, DM, Malamuth, NM (1996): *Sex, Power, Conflict: Evolutionary and Feminist Perspectives.* New York: Oxford University Press.
Butler, AC, Chapman, JE, Forman, EM, Beck, AT (2006): The empirical status of cognitive-behavioral therapy: a review of meta-analyses. *Clinical Psychology Review* 26: 17–31.
Cacioppo, JT, Patrick, W (2008): *Loneliness: Human Nature and the Need for Social Connection.* New York: Norton.
Cain, NM, Pincus, AL, Ansell, EB (2008): Narcissism at the crossroads: phenotypic description of pathological narcissism across clinical theory, social/personality psychology, and psychiatric diagnosis. *Clinical Psychology Review* 28: 638–656.
Campbell, J (1949): *The Hero with a Thousand Faces.* New York: Pantheon Books.
Campbell, WK (1999): Narcissism and romantic attraction. *Journal of Personality and Social Psychology* 77: 1254–1270.
Campbell, WK, Miller, JD, Buffardi, LE (2010): The United States and the "culture of narcissism": an examination of perceptions of national character. *Social Psychological and Personality Science* 1: 222–229.
Campbell, WK, Miller, JD (Eds) (2011): *Handbook of Narcissism and Narcissistic Personality Disorde*r. New York: Wiley.
Caplan, E (1998): *Mind Games: American Culture and the Birth of Psychotherapy.* Berkeley: University of California Press.
Cardoso-Zoppe, EHC, Schoueri, P, Castro, M, Neto, FL (2009): Teaching psychodynamics to psychiatric residents through psychiatric outpatient interviews *Academic Psychiatry* 33: 51–55.
Carlat, D (2010): *Unhinged.* New York, Free Press.
Cassidy, J, Shaver, PR (Eds) (2009): *Handbook of Attachment: Theory, Research and Clinical Aspects,* 2nd edition. New York: Guilford.
Chambless, DL, Hollon, SD (1998): Defining empirically supported therapies. *Journal of Consulting and Clinical Psychology* 66: 7–18.
Cherlin, AJ (2004): *Public & Private Families: An Introduction.* New York: McGraw Hill.
Cherlin, AJ, Furstenberg, FF, Chase-Lansdale, P, Lindsay, K, Kiernan, K (1991): Longitudinal studies of effects of divorce on children in Great Britain and the United States. *Science* 252: 1386–1389.
Clarkin, JF, & Levy, KN (2003): Influence of client variables on psychotherapy. In M. Lambert (Ed.), Handbook of Psychotherapy and Behavior Change (5th ed.). New York: Wiley & Sons, pp. 194–226.
Cochran, SD, Mays, VM (2000): Lifetime prevalence of suicidal symptoms and affective disorders among men reporting same-sex sexual partners: Results from the NHANES III. *American Journal of Public Health* 90: 573–578.
Cohen, P, Crawford, TN, Johnson, JG, Kasen, S (2005): The children in the community study: developmental course of personality disorder. *Journal of Personality Disorders* 19: 466–486.
Cohler, BJ, Galatzer-Lev, RM (2000): *The Course of Gay and Lesbian Lives.* Chicago: University of Chicago Press.
Comfort, A (1972): *The Joy of Sex.* New York: Simon and Schuster.
Compton WM, Helzer JE, Hwu HG, Yeh EK, McEvoy L, Tipp JE, Spitznagel E (1991): New methods in cross-cultural psychiatry: comparing rates of

psychiatric illness in Taiwan to rates in the United States. *American Journal of Psychiatry* 148: 1697–1704.
Coontz, S (2005): *Marriage, A History: From Obedience to Intimacy, or How Love Conquered Marriage.* New York: Penguin.
Cosmides, L, Tooby, J (2008): *Universal Minds: Explaining the New Science of Evolutionary Psychology.* London: Weidenfeld & Nicolson.
Costa, PT, Widiger, TA (Eds) (2001): *Personality Disorders and the Five Factor Model of Personality* (2nd ed.). Washington, DC: American Psychological Association.
Costa, PT, Jr, Terracciano, A, McCrae, RR (2001): Gender differences in personality traits across cultures: robust and surprising findings. *Journal of Personality and Social Psychology* 81: 322–331.
Crews, F (1995): *The Memory Wars.* New York: New York Review of Books Press.
Crits-Christoph, P, Barber, JP (Eds) (1991): *Handbook of Short-term Dynamic Psychotherapy.* New York: Basic Books.
Cross, SE, Madson, L (1997): Models of the self, self-construals and gender. *Psychological Bulletin* 122: 5–37.
Cummings, NA, Sayama, M (1995): *Focused Psychotherapy: A Casebook of Brief, Intermittent Psychotherapy Throughout the Life Cycle.* Philadelphia: Brunner/Mazel.
Cushman, P (1995): *Constructing the Self, Constructing America: A Cultural History of Psychotherapy.* New York: Addison-Wesley.
Dawes, RM (1994): *House of Cards: Psychology and Psychotherapy Built on Myth.* New York: Free Press.
Decker, HS (2008): Psychoanalysis in Central Europe: the interplay of psychoanalysis and culture, In ER Wallace IV (Ed.), *History of Psychiatry and Medical Psychology.* New York: Springer, pp. 587–628.
Dembling, S (2005): *The Making of Dr. Phil: The Straight-Talking True Story of Everyone's Favorite Therapist.* New York: Wiley.
De Silva, MJ, McKenzie, K, Harpham, T, Huttly, S (2005): Social capital and mental illness: a systematic review. *Journal of Epidemiology and Community Health* 59: 619–627.
DeWall, CN, Pond, RS, Campbell, WK, Twenge, J (2011): Tuning in to psychological change: linguistic markers of psychological traits and emotions over time in popular U.S. song lyrics. *Psychology of Aesthetics, Creativity, and the Arts,* 5: 200–207 doi: 10.1037/a0023195.
Diamant, L, McNulty, RD (Eds) (1995): *The Psychology of Sexual Orientation, Behavior, and Identity: A Handbook.* Westport, CT: Greenwood Press.
Dineen, T. (1996): *Manufacturing Victims: What the Psychology Industry is Doing to People.* Westmount, Canada: Robert Davies.
Doherty, WJ, Simmons, DS (1996): Clinical practice patterns of marriage and family therapists: a national survey of therapists and their clients. *Journal of Marital and Family Therapy* 22: 9–25.
Doidge, N, Simon, B, Brauer, L, Grant, DC, First, M, Brunshaw, J, Lancee, WJ, Stevens, A, Oldham, JM, Mosher, P (2002): Psychoanalytic patients in the U.S., Canada, and Australia: I. DSM-III-R disorders, indications, previous treatment, medications, and length of treatment. *Journal of the American Psychoanalytic Association* 50: 575–614.
Dolnick, E (1998): *Madness on the Couch.* New York: Simon and Schuster.

Dunn, J, Plomin, R (1993), *Separate Lives: Why Siblings Are So Different.* Washington DC: American Psychological Association.

Dunn, R, Schwebel, A (1995): Meta-analytic review of marital therapy outcome research. *Journal of Family Psychology* 9: 58–68.

Durkheim, E (1897/1997): *Suicide.* New York, Free Press.

Durvasula, S, Lysonski, S, Watson, J (2001): Does vanity describe other cultures? A cross-cultural examination of the vanity scale. *Journal of Consumer Affairs* 35: 180–199.

Dush, CM, Kamp, D, Cohan, CL, Amato, PR (2003): The relationship between cohabitation and marital quality and stability: change across cohorts? *Journal of Marriage and Family* 65: 539–549.

Ehrenberg, A (2010): *The Weariness of the Self: Diagnosing the History of Depression in the Contemporary Age.* Montreal: McGill-Queens University Press.

Eksteins, M (1989). *Rites of Spring: The Great War and the Birth of the Modern Age.* Boston: Houghton Mifflin.

Elder, G (1974): *Children of the Great Depression.* Chicago: University of Chicago Press.

Elkin, I, Shea, T, Watkins, JT, Imber, SD (1989): National institute of mental health treatment of depression collaborative research program: general effectiveness of treatments. *Archives of General Psychiatry* 46: 971–982.

Ellenberger, HE (1970): *The Discovery of the Unconscious. The History and Evolution of Dynamic Psychiatry*: New York: Basic Books.

Elliott, C (2003): *Better Than Well: American Medicine Meets the American Dream.* New York: Norton.

Ellis, A (2001): *Overcoming Destructive Beliefs, Feelings, and Behaviors: New Directions for Rational Emotive Behavior Therapy.* New York: Prometheus Books.

Engel, G (1980): The clinical application of the biopsychosocial model. *American Journal of Psychiatry* 137: 535–544.

Engel, J (2008): *American Therapy.* New York: Penguin.

Engels, F (1884/1972): *The Origin of the Family, Private Property and the State.* New York: Pathfinder.

Epstein, WB (1995): *The Illusion of Psychotherapy.* London and New York: Transaction Publishers.

Epstein, WB (2006): *Psychotherapy as Religion: The Civil Divine In America.* Las Vegas, NV: University of Nevada Press.

Erikson, E (1950): *Childhood and Society.* New York: Norton.

Etzioni, A (1993): *The Spirit of Community: Rights, Responsibilities and the Communitarian Agenda.* New York: Crown.

Eysenck, H (1952): The effects of psychotherapy: an evaluation. *Journal of Consulting Psychology* 16: 319–324.

Festinger, L (1957): *A Theory of Cognitive Dissonance.* Stanford, CA: Stanford University Press.

Finkel, EJ, Campbell, WK, Buffardi, LE, Kumashiro, M, Rusbult, E (2009): The metamorphosis of narcissus: communal activation promotes relationship commitment among narcissists. *Personality and Social Psychology Bulletin* 35: 1271.

Finkelhor, D, Jones, L (2006): Why have child maltreatment and victimization declined? *Journal of Social Issues* 62: 685–715.

Fischer, C (2010): *Made in America.* Chicago: University of Chicago Press.

Fisher, H (2004): *Why We Love—the Nature and Chemistry of Romantic Love.* New York: Henry Holt.
Fisher, S, Greenberg, R (1996): *Freud Scientifically Appraised: Testing the Theories and Therapy.* New York: Wiley.
Fisher, WH (Ed.) (2004): *Research on Employment for Persons with Severe Mental Illness.* Bingley, UK: Emerald Group Publishing.
Fonagy, P (2001) *Attachment Theory and Psychoanalysis.* New York: Other Press.
Foster, JD, Campbell, WK, Twenge, JM (2003): Individual differences in narcissism: inflated self-views across the lifespan and around the world. *Journal of Research in Personality* 37: 469–486.
Foucault, M (2001): *Madness and Civilization: A History of Insanity in the Age of Reason,* Richard Howard (Trans.) New York: Routledge.
Frank, JD, Frank, JB (1991): *Persuasion and Healing,* 3rd edition. Baltimore: Johns Hopkins.
Frazier, SL, Formoso, D, Birman, D, Atkins, MS (2008): Closing the research to practice gap: redefining feasibility. *Clinical Psychology: Science and Practice.* 15: 125–129.
Freeman, D (1983): *Margaret Mead and Samoa.* Cambridge, MA: Harvard University Press.
Freud, S. (1957, originally published 1896): The aetiology of hysteria. In J. Strachey (Ed. & Trans.), *The Standard Edition of the Complete Psychological Works of Sigmund Freud.* London: Hogarth Press. 3, 191–224.
Freud, S (1959, originally published 1914): On Narcissism: An Introduction, in *The Standard Edition of the Psychological Works of Sigmund Freud,* London, Hogarth Press 14: 67–102.
Freud, S (1962, originally published 1937): Analysis terminable and interminable: In *The Standard Edition of the Psychological Works of Sigmund Freud* London, Hogarth Press 23: 216–254.
Freud, S (1989, originally published 1930): *Civilization and Its Discontents.* New York: Norton.
Fromm, E (1941): *Escape from Freedom.* London: Routledge.
Fromm, E (1956): *The Art of Loving.* New York: Harper and Row.
Furedi, F (2004): *Therapy Culture: Cultivating Vulnerability in an Uncertain Age.* London: Routledge.
Furedi, F (2005): Interview with Mark Thwaite, *Ready Steady Book* http://www.readysteadybook.com/Article.aspx?page=furedi, accessed October 2010.
Furedi, F (2008): *Paranoid Parenting,* 2nd edition. London: Continuum Press.
Furet, F (1999): *The Passing of an Illusion.* Chicago: University of Chicago Press.
Furstenberg, FF (2000): The sociology of adolescence and youth in the 1990s: a critical commentary. *Journal of Marriage and the Family* 62: 896–910.
Gabbard, GO (2005): *Psychodynamic Psychiatry In Clinical Practice.* Washington DC: American Psychiatric Publishing.
Gabbard, GO, Gabbard, KA (1999): *Psychiatry and the Cinema,* 2nd edition. Washington DC: American Psychiatric Press.
Gabbard, GO, Lazar, SG, Hornberger, J, Spiegel, D (1997): The economic impact of psychotherapy: a review. *American Journal of Psychiatry* 154: 147–155.
Gardner, M (1957): *Fads and Fallacies in the Name of Science.* New York: Dover.

Garfield, SL (1994): Research on client variables in psychotherapy, In Garfield, SL, Bergin, AE (Eds), *Handbook of Psychotherapy and Behavior Change,* 4th edition, New York: John Wiley, pp.190–228.

Gaston, L, Thompson, L, Gallagher, D, Cournoyer, LG, Gagnon, R (1998): Alliance, techniques, and their interactions in predicting outcome of behavioral, cognitive, and brief dynamic therapy. *Psychotherapy Research* 8: 190–209.

Gauvreau, M (2007): *The Catholic Origins of Quebec's Quiet Revolution, 1931–1970.* Montreal: McGill-Queen's University Press.

Gellner, E (1993): *The Psychoanalytic Movement*, second edition. London: Fontana.

Gergen, KJ (1991): *The Saturated Self: Dilemmas of Identity in Contemporary Society.* New York: Basic.

Giddens, A (1991): *The Consequences of Modernity.* Stanford, CA: Stanford University Press.

Giddens, A. (1998): *Conversations with Anthony Giddens: Making Sense of Modernity.* Stanford, CA: Stanford University Press.

Glick, ID (1980): *Marital and Family Therapy.* New York: Grune & Stratton.

Goldberg, S (1973): *The Inevitability of Patriarchy.* New York: William Morrow.

Goldberg, S (1993): *Why Men Rule.* Chicago: Open Court Publishing.

Goldenberg, I, Goldenberg, H (1999) *Family Therapy: An Overview,* 5th edition. New York: Wadsworth.

Gottman, JM, Driver, J, Tabares, A (2002): Building the sound marital house: an empirically derived couple therapy. In AS Gurman, NS Jacobson (Eds.), *Clinical handbook of couple therapy* (3rd edition, pp. 373–399). New York: Guilford Press.

Grant, BF, Dawson, DA, Stinson, FS, Chou, P, Dufour, MC, Pickering, RP (2004): The 12-month prevalence and trends in DSM–IV alcohol abuse and dependence: United States, 1991–1992 and 2001–2001. *Drug and Alcohol Dependence* 74: 223–234.

Gross, P, Levitt, N (1994): *Higher Superstition: The Academic Left and Its Quarrels with Science.* Baltimore: Johns Hopkins Press.

Gross, MA (1978): *The Psychological Society.* New York: Harper Collins.

Gross, P, Levitt, N, Lewis, MW (1997): *The Flight from Science and Reason.* New York: New York Academy of Science.

Grosskurth, P (1984): *Melanie Klein: Her World and Her Work.* New York: Knopf.

Grunbaum, A (1984): *The Foundations of Psychoanalysis*, Berkeley, CA: University of California Press.

Gunderson, JG, Ronningstam, E, Smith, L (1995): Narcissistic personality disorder. In WJ Livesley (Ed.), *The DSM- IV Personality Disorders.* New York: Guilford, pp. 201–212.

Guntrip, H (1985): *Psychoanalytic Theory, Therapy, and the Self.* New York: Karnac Books.

Haferkamp, H, Smelser, NJ (Eds) (1992): *Social Change and Modernity.* Berkeley: University of California Press.

Hale, R (1995): *The Rise and Crisis of Psychoanalysis in the United States.* New York: Oxford University Press.

Hall, GS (1904): *Adolescence: Its Psychology and Its Relations to Physiology, Anthropology, Sociology, Sex, Crime, Religion, and Education*, 2 vols. New York: Appleton.

Halpert, E (1972): The effect of insurance on psychoanalytic treatment. *Journal of the American Psychoanalytic Association* 20: 122–133.

Harris, JR (1998): *The Nurture Assumption.* New York: Free Press.

Harris, JR (2006): *No Two Alike: Human Nature and Human Individuality*. New York: Norton.
Hartmann, H (1964): *Ego Psychology & the Problem of Adaptation*. New York: International Universities Press.
Hayes, SC, Strosahl, K, Wilson, KG (1999): *Acceptance and Commitment Therapy: An Experiential Approach to Behavior Change*. New York: Guilford Press.
Healy, D (2002): *The Creation of Psychopharmacology*. Cambridge, MA: Harvard University Press.
Helzer, JE, Hwu, HG, Yeh, EK, McEvoy L, Tipp, JE, Spitznagel, EL (1991): New methods in cross-cultural psychiatry: psychiatric illness in Taiwan and the United States. *American Journal of Psychiatry* 148: 1697–1704.
Henry, WE, Sims, JH, Spray, SL (1971): *The Fifth Profession*. San Francisco: Jossey Bass.
Henry, WE, Sims, JH, Spray, SL (1973): *The Public and Private Lives of Psychotherapists*. San Francisco: Jossey Bass.
Herman, JL (1992): *Trauma and Recovery*. New York: Basic.
Hetherington, EM, Cox, M, Cox, R (1985): Long-term effects of divorce and remarriage on the adjustment of children. *Journal of the American Academy of Child & Adolescent Psychiatry* 24: 518–530.
Hewitt, JP (1998): *The Myth of Self-Esteem*. New York: Palgrave Macmillan.
Hofmann, SG, Sawyer, AT, Fang, A (2010): The empirical status of the "new wave" of cognitive behavioral therapy. *Psychiatric Clinics of North America* 33: 701–710.
Hogarty, GE, Schooler, NR, Baker, RW (1997): Efficacy versus effectiveness. *Psychiatric Services* 48: 1107.
Hoglend, P, Bøgwald, KJ, Amlo, S, Marble, A, Ulberg, R, Sjaastad, MC, Sørbye, O, Heyerdahl, O, Johansson, P (2008): Transference interpretations in dynamic psychotherapy: do they really yield sustained effects? *American Journal of Psychiatry* 165: 763–771.
Holmes, D (1990): The evidence for repression: an examination of sixty years of research, In J Singer (Ed.), *Repression and Dissociation: Implications for Personality Theory, Psychopathology, and Health*. Chicago: University of Chicago Press, pp. 85–102.
Horton, RS, Bleau, G, Drwecki, D (2006). Parenting narcissus: What are the links between parenting and narcissism? *Journal of Personality* 74: 345–352.
Horton, RS (2011): Parenting and narcissism, In WK Campbell, J Miller (Eds), *Handbook of Narcissism and Narcissistic Personality Disorde*r. New York: Wiley, pp. 181–190.
Horwitz, AV, Wakefield, JC (2007): *The Loss of Sadness: How Psychiatry Transformed Normal Sorrow into Depressive Disorder*. New York: Oxford University Press.
Horwitz, L (1974): *Clinical Prediction in Psychotherapy*. New York: Aronson.
House, JS, Landis, KR, Umberson, D (1988): Social relationships and health. *Science* 241: 540–545.
Hout, M, Fischer, C (2002): Explaining the rise of Americans with no religious preference. *American Sociological Review* 67: 165–190.
Howard, KI, Kopta, SM, Krause, MS, Orlinsky, DE (1986): The dose-effect relationship to psychotherapy. *American Psychologist* 41: 159–164.
Howard, KI, Cornille, TA, Lyons, JS, Vessey, JT, Lueger, RJ, Saunders, SM (1996): Patterns of mental health service utilization. *Archives of General Psychiatry* 53: 696–703.

Hrdy, SB (2009): *Mothers and Others: The Evolutionary Origins of Mutual Understanding*. Cambridge, MA: Harvard University Press.

Hubble, MA, Duncan, BL, Miller, SD (Eds) (1999): *The Heart and Soul of Change: What Works in Therapy*. Washington DC: American Psychological Association.

Hunsley, J, Rumstein-McKean, O (1999): Improving psychotherapeutic services via randomized clinical trials, treatment manuals, and component analysis designs. *Journal of Clinical Psychology* 55: 1507–1517.

Hunter, JD (2000): *The Death of Character: Moral Education without Good or Evil*. New York: Basic Books.

Ingelhardt, RF, Abramson, P (1995): *Value Change in Global Perspective*. Ann Arbor: University of Michigan Press.

Jang, KL, Livesley, WJ, Vernon, PA, Jackson, DN (1996): Heritability of personality traits: a twin study. *Acta Psychiatrica Scandinavica* 94: 438–444.

Janov, A (1970): *The Primal Scream*. New York: Putnam.

Johnson, P (1990): *The Birth of the Modern*. New York: Harper Collins.

Jones, E (1953): *The Life and Work of Sigmund Freud: The Formative Years and the Great Discoveries*, 1856–1900, Vol. 1. New York: Basic Books.

Jones, EE, Harris, VA (1967): The attribution of attitudes. *Journal of Experimental Social Psychology* 3: 1–24.

Jung, CG (1996): *The Essential Jung*, In: Anthony Storr (Ed.). New York: MJF Books.

Kagan, J (1998): *Three Seductive Ideas*. Cambridge MA: Harvard University Press.

Kagan, J (2008): *What is Emotion*? New Haven: Yale University Press.

Kalmijn, M (2007): Gender differences in the effects of divorce, widowhood and remarriage on intergenerational support: does marriage protect fathers? *Social Forces* 8: 1079–1104.

Kaminer, W (1992): *I'm Dysfunctional, You're Dysfunctional: The Recovery Movement and Other Self-Help Fashions*. New York: Addison-Wesley.

Kardiner, A (1977): *My Analysis with Freud*. New York: Norton.

Kazdin, AE (2008): Evidence-based treatment and practice: new opportunities to bridge clinical research and practice, enhance the knowledge base, and improve patient care. *American Psychologist* 63: 146–159.

Kelly, EL, Conley, JJ (1987): Personality and compatibility: a prospective analysis of marital stability and marital satisfaction. *Journal of Personality and Social Psychology* 52: 27–40.

Kent, S (2001): *From Slogans to Mantras: Social Protest and Religious Conversion in the Late Vietnam War Era*. Syracuse, NY: Syracuse University Press.

Kernberg, OF (1976): *Borderline Conditions and Pathological Narcissism*. New York: Jason Aronson.

Kernberg, OF (1987): *Severe Personality Disorders*. New York: Basic.

Kernberg, OF (1995): *Love Relations: Normality and Pathology*. New Haven: Yale University Press.

Kernberg, OF, Coyne, L, Appelbaum, A, Horwitz, L, Voth, H (1972): Final report of the Menninger psychotherapy research project. *Bulletin* of *the Menninger Clinic* 36: 1–275.

Kessler, RC, Merikangas, KR, Berglund, P, Eaton, WW, Koretz, DS, Walters, EE (2003): Mild disorders should not be eliminated from the DSM-V. *Archives of General Psychiatry* 60: 1117–1122.

Kessler, RC, Chiu, WT, Demler, O, Merikangas, KR, Walters, EE (2005a): Prevalence, severity, and comorbidity of 12-month DSM-IV disorders in the National Comorbidity Survey Replication. *Archives of General Psychiatry* 62: 617–627.

Kessler, RC, Demler, O, Frank, RG, Olfson, M, Pincus, HA, Walters, EE, Wang, P, Wells, KB, Zaslavsky, AM (2005b): Prevalence and treatment of mental disorders, 1990 to 2003. *New England Journal of Medicine* 352: 2515–2523.

Kihlstrom, JF (1999): The psychological unconscious. In LR Pervin, O John (Eds). Handbook of personality, 2nd edition, pp. 424–442. New York: Guilford.

Kinsey, AC, Pomeroy, WB, Martin, CE (1948): *Sexual Behavior in the Human Male.* Philadelphia, PA: W.B. Saunders.

Kinsey, AC, Pomeroy, WB, Martin, CE, Gebhard, PH (1953): *Sexual Behavior in the Human Female.* Philadelphia, PA: W.B. Saunders.

Kirmayer, LJ (2004): The cultural diversity of healing: meaning, metaphor and mechanism. *British Medical Bulletin* 69 (1): 33–48.

Kirmayer, LJ (2007): Psychotherapy and the cultural concept of the person. *Transcultural Psychiatry* 44: 232–257.

Kirmayer, LJ, Robbins, JM (1991): Concepts of somatization, In LJ Kirmayer, JM Robbins (Eds), *Current Concepts of Somatization.* Washington DC: American Psychiatric Press.

Kirsch, I, Brett, J, Deacon, TB, Huedo-Medina, A, Moore, TJ, Johnson, BT (2008): Initial severity and antidepressant benefits: a meta-analysis of data submitted to the Food and Drug Administration. *PLOS Medicine* 5 (2): e45. doi:10.1371/journal.pmed.0050045.

Klein, M (1946): *Envy and Gratitude.* New York: International Universities Press.

Kleinman, A (1988): *Rethinking Psychiatry: From Cultural Category to Personal Experience.* New York: The Free Press.

Klerman, GL, Weissman, MM (1989): Increasing rates of depression. JAMA 261: 2229–2235.

Klerman, GL, Weissman, MM (Eds) (1993): *New Applications of the Interpersonal Therapy of Depression.* Washington DC: American Psychiatric Press.

Knekt, P, Lindfors, O, Harkanen, T, Valikoski, M, Virtala, E, Laaksonen, MA, Marttunen, M, Kaipainen, M, Renlund, C (2008): Randomized trial on the effectiveness of long and short-term psychodynamic psychotherapy and solution-focused therapy on psychiatric symptoms during a 3-year follow-up. *Psychological Medicine* 38: 689–703.

Koenig, HG (2001): Religion and medicine II: religion, mental health, and related behaviors. *International Journal of Psychiatry in Medicine* 31: 97–109.

Kohut, H (1970): *The Analysis of the Self.* New York: International Universities Press.

Kohut, H (1977): *The Restoration of the Self.* New York: International Universities Press.

Kohut, H (1984): *How Does Analysis Cure?* In A Goldberg, P Stepansky (Eds). Chicago: University of Chicago Press.

Konrath, SA, O'Brien, E, Hsing, C (2011): Changes in dispositional empathy in American college students over time: a meta-analysis. *Personality and Social Psychology Review* 15: 180–198.

Kopta, SM, Howard, KI, Lowry, JL, Beutler, LE (1994): Patterns of symptomatic recovery in psychotherapy. *Journal of Consulting and Clinical Psychology* 62: 1009–1016.

Kovel, J (1976): *A Complete Guide to Therapy: From Psychoanalysis to Behavior Modification*. New York: Pantheon.
Kramer, P (1997): *Should You Leave? A Psychiatrist Explores Intimacy and Autonomy—and the Nature of Advice*. New York: Penguin.
Krueger, RF (1999): The structure of common mental disorders. *Archives of General Psychiatry* 56: 921–926.
Kuhn, TA (1970): *The Structure of Scientific Revolutions*, second edition. Chicago: University of Chicago Press.
Kurdek, LA (1998): Relationship outcomes and their predictors: longitudinal evidence from heterosexual married, gay cohabiting, and lesbian cohabiting couples. *Journal of Marriage and the Family* 60: 553–568.
Kutcher, SP, Szumilas, M (2008): Youth suicide prevention. *Canadian Medical Association Journal,* 178: 282–285.
Lambert, M (Ed.) (2003): *Bergin and Garfield's Handbook of Psychotherapy and Behavior Change*. New York: Wiley.
Langstrom, N, Hanson, RK (2006): High rates of sexual behavior in the general population: correlates and predictors. *Archives of Sexual Behavior* 35: 37–52.
Larsen, RJ, Buss, DM (2008): *Personality Psychology: Domains of Knowledge about Human Nature,* 3rd edition. New York: McGraw Hill.
Lasch, C (1979): *The Culture of Narcissism*. New York: Warner.
Lasch, C (1977): *Haven in a Heartless World: The Family Besieged,* New York: Norton.
Laumann, EO, Kolata, G, Gagnon, JH, Michael, RT (1994): *Sex in America: A Definitive Survey*. New York: Little, Brown.
Laws, RD, O'Donohue, W (Eds) (1997): *Sexual Deviance*. New York, Guilford.
Lazar, SG (Ed.) (2010): *Psychotherapy Is Worth It: A Comprehensive Review of Its Cost-Effectiveness*. Washington DC: American Psychiatric Publishing.
Leichsenring, F, Rabung, S, Leibing, E (2004): The efficacy of short-term psychodynamic psychotherapy in specific psychiatric disorders: a meta-analysis. *Archives of General Psychiatry* 61: 1208–1216.
Leichsenring, F, Rabung, S (2008): Effectiveness of long-term psychodynamic psychotherapy: A meta-analysis. *JAMA* 300:1551–1565.
Leichsenring, F, Rabung, S (2011): Long-term psychodynamic psychotherapy in complex mental disorders: update of a meta-analysis. *British Journal of Psychiatry* 199: 15–22.
Leighton, DC, Harding, JS, Macklin, DB (1963). *The Character of Danger: Psychiatric Symptoms in Selected Communities*. New York: Basic.
Lerner, D (1958): *The Passing of Traditional Society.* New York: Free Press.
Lester, D (1996): The impact of unemployment on marriage and divorce. *Journal of Divorce & Remarriage* 25: 151–154.
Levy, DA, Nail, PR (1993): Contagion: a theoretical and empirical review and reconceptualization. *Genetic, Social, & General Psychology Monographs* 119: 233–284.
Lieberman, MA, Yalom, ID (1973): *Encounter Groups: First Facts*. New York: Basic Books.
Lilienfeld, SO, Lynn, SJ, Lohr, JM (2001): *Science and Pseudoscience in Clinical Psychology,* Washington DC: American Psychological Association.
Lilla, M (2007): *The Stillborn God: Religion, Politics, and the Modern West.* New York, Knopf.

Lindberg, LD, Singh, S (2008): Sexual behavior of single adult American women. *Perspectives on Sexual and Reproductive Health* 40: 27–33.
Linehan, MM (1993): *Dialectical Behavior Therapy for Borderline Personality Disorder.* New York: Guilford.
Lloyd, G (2008): *Providence Lost.* Cambridge: Harvard University Press.
Loftus, E, Davis, D (2006): Recovered memories. *Annual Review of Clinical Psychology* 2: 469–498.
Luborsky, L, Singer, B, Luborsky, L (1975): Comparative studies of psychotherapy: is it true that "everyone has won and all shall have prizes"? *Archives of General Psychiatry* 41: 165–180.
Luborsky, L, Luborsky, E (2006): *Research and Psychotherapy: The Vital Link.* Lanham MD: Jason Aronson.
Luhrmann, TM (2000): *Of Two Minds: An Anthropologist Looks at American Psychiatry.* New York: Vintage Books.
Lyons, LC, Woods, PJ (1991): The efficacy of rational-emotive therapy: A quantitative review of the outcome research. *Clinical Psychology Review* 11: 357–369.
MacKenzie, KR (1996): The time-limited psychotherapies: An overview. *American Psychiatric Press Review of Psychiatry* 15: 11–21.
Malcolm, J (1982): *Psychoanalysis: The Impossible Profession*, New York: Vintage.
Mann, J (1973): *Time-limited psychotherapy.* Cambridge, MA: Harvard University Press.
Markus, H, Kitayama, A (1991): Culture and the self: implications for cognition, emotion, and motivation. *Psychological Review* 98: 224–253.
Maslow, A (1943): A theory of motivation. *Psychological Review* 50: 370–396.
McCallum, M, Piper, WE (Eds) (1997): *Psychological Mindedness: A Contemporary Understanding.* Munich, Germany: Lawrence Erlbaum Associates.
McCullough, ME, Emmons, RA, Kilpatrick, SD, Mooney, CN (2003): Narcissists as "victims": the role of narcissism in the perception of transgressions. *Personality and Social Psychology Bulletin*, 29, 885–893.
McGoldrick, M, Giordano, J., Garcia-Preto, N (2005): *Ethnicity and Family Therapy*, third edition. New York: Guilford.
McHugh, PR (2008): *Try to Remember.* Baltimore: Johns Hopkins Press.
McLanahan, S, Sandefur, G (1994): *Growing Up With a Single Parent: What Hurts, What Helps.* Cambridge: Harvard University Press.
McNally, RL (2003): *Remembering Trauma.* Cambridge MA: Harvard University Press.
McPherson, M, Smith-Lovin, L, Brashears, M (2006): Social isolation in America: changes in core discussion groups over two decades. *American Sociological Review* 71: 353–375.
Mead, M (1928/2001): *Coming of Age in Samoa: A Psychological Study of Primitive Youth for Western Civilization.* New York: Perennial Classics.
Mead, N, Lester, H, Chew-Graham, C, Gask, L (2010): Effects of befriending on depressive symptoms and distress: systematic review and meta-analysis. *British Journal of Psychiatry* 196: 96–101.
Meszaros, I (1992): *Marx's theory of Alienation*, 3rd edition. London: Merlin Press.
Miller, A (1984): *Prisoners of Childhood: The Drama of the Gifted Child and the Search for the True Self.* New York: Farrar, Strauss, and Giroux.
Miller, G (2009): *Spent: Sex, Evolution and Consumer Behavior.* New York: Viking.

Miller, JD, Campbell, K, Pilkonis, P (2007): Narcissistic personality disorder: relations with distress and functional impairment. *Comprehensive Psychiatry* 48: 170–177.
Miller, JD, Campbell, K (2008): Comparing clinical and social-personality conceptualizations of narcissism. *Journal of Personality* 76: 449–476.
Miller, S, Duncan, H (1997): *Escape from Babel: Toward a Unifying Language for Psychotherapy Practice*. New York: Norton.
Miller, WR, Rollnick, S (2002): *Motivational Interviewing*, 2nd edition. New York: Guilford.
Millon, T (1993): Borderline personality disorder: a psychosocial epidemic, In J Paris (Ed.), *Borderline Personality Disorder: Etiology and Treatment*. Washington DC: American Psychiatric Press, pp. 197–210.
Minuchin, S (1974): *Families and Family Therapy*. Cambridge, MA: Harvard University Press.
Mitchell, JT (1983): When disaster strikes: the critical incident stress debriefing process. *Journal of Emergency Medical Services* 8: 36–39.
Mojtabai, R (2007): Americans' attitudes toward mental health treatment seeking: 1990–2003. *Psychiatric Services* 58: 642–651.
Mojtabai, R (2008): Increase in antidepressant medication in the US adult population between 1990 and 2003. *Psychotherapy and Psychosomatics* 77: 83–92.
Mojtabai, R, Olfson, M (2008): National trends in psychotherapy by office-based psychiatrists. *Archives of General Psychiatry* 65: 962–970.
Mojtabai, R, Olfson M, Sampson, NA, Jin, R, Druss, B, Wang, PS, Wells, KB, Pincus, HA, Kessler, RC (2010): Barriers to mental health treatment: results from the National Comorbidity Survey Replication. *Psychological Medicine*, 41: 1751–1761 doi: 10.1017/S0033291710002291.
Moncrieff, J (2008): *The Myth of the Chemical Cure*. London: Palgrave Macmillan.
Monkkonen, E (2001): New standards for historical violence research. *Crime, History, Society* 5: 5–26.
Morrell, S, Page, A, Taylor, R (2007): The decline in Australian young male suicide. *Social Science & Medicine* 64: 747–754.
Moskowitz, ES (2001): *In Therapy We Trust: America's Obsession with Self-Fulfillment*. Baltimore: Johns Hopkins Press.
Muncy, RL (1973): *Sex and Marriage in Utopian Communities: 19th Century America*. Bloomington: Indiana Press, 1973.
Murdock, GP (1949): *Social Structure*. New York: The Free Press.
Murphy, HBM (1982): *Comparative Psychiatry*. New York: Springer.
Nathan, D (2011): *Sibyl Exposed*. New York: Simon and Schuster.
Nathanson, P, Young, KK (2006): *Spreading Misandry: The Teaching of Contempt for Men in Popular Culture*. Montreal: McGill-Queen's University Press.
Nesse, RM, Williams, GC (1995): *Why We Get Sick: The New Science of Darwinian Medicine*. New York: Times Books.
Newton-Howes, G, Tyrer, P, Johnson, T (2006): Personality disorder and the outcome of depression: meta-analysis of published studies. *British Journal of Psychiatry* 188: 13–20.
Nisbett, R (2003): *The Geography of Thought: How Asians and Westerners Think Differently – and Why*. New York: Free Press.
Norcross, JC, Goldfried, MR (2005): *Handbook of Psychotherapy Integration*, 2nd edition, New York: Oxford University Press.

Norris, P, Inglehart, R (2004): *Sacred and Secular: Religion and Politics Worldwide.* Cambridge UK: Cambridge University Press.

North, M (1972): *The Secular Priests.* London George Allen & Unwin.

O'Donnell, M (1997): *A Sceptic's Medical Dictionary.* London: BMJ Publishing Group.

Offer, D, Offer, J (1975): Three developmental routes through normal male adolescence. *Adolescent Psychiatry* 4: 121–141.

Ofshe, R, Watters, E (1994): *Making Monsters: False Memories, Psychotherapy, and Sexual Hysteria.* New York: Scribner.

Ogrodniczuk, JS, Piper, WE, Joyce, AS, McCallum, M (1999): Transference Interpretations in Short-Term Dynamic Psychotherapy. *Journal of Nervous and Mental Diseases* 187: 571–578.

Ogrodniczuk, JS, Piper, WE, Joyce, AS, Steinberg, PI, Duggal, S (2009): Interpersonal problems associated with narcissism among psychiatric outpatients. *Journal of Psychiatric Research* 43, 837–842.

Olfson, M, Pincus, HA (1994): Outpatient psychotherapy in the United States, I: Volume, costs, and user characteristics. *American Journal of Psychiatry* 151: 1281–1288.

Olfson, M, Marcus, SC, Druss, B, Pincus, HA (2002): National trends in the use of outpatient psychotherapy. *American Journal of Psychiatry* 159: 1914–1920.

Olfson, M, Marcus, SC (2010): National trends in outpatient psychotherapy. *American Journal of Psychiatry* 167: 1456–1463.

Orlinsky, DE, Grawe, K, Parks, BK (1994): Process and outcome in psychotherapy—noch einmal, In AE Bergin, SL Garfield, (Eds), *Handbook of Psychotherapy and Behavior Change.* New York: Wiley, pp. 270–379.

Osler, W (1898): *The Principles and Practice of Medicine.* New York: Applelton.

Paris, J (1991): The deathly embrace: the fate of symbiosis in marriage. *Journal of the American Academy of Psychoanalysis* 19: 316–320.

Paris, J (1996a): *Social Factors in the Personality Disorders.* Cambridge, UK: Cambridge University Press.

Paris, J (1996b): A critical review of recovered memories in psychotherapy: trauma and memory. *Canadian Journal of Psychiatry* 41: 201–205.

Paris, J (2000): *Myths of Childhood.* Philadelphia, PA: Brunner/Mazzel.

Paris, J (2004): Sociocultural factors in the treatment of personality disorders, In J Magnavita (Ed.), *Handbook of Personality Disorders: Theory and Practice.* New York: Wiley, pp. 135–147.

Paris, J (2005): *The Fall of an Icon: Psychoanalysis and Academic Psychiatry.* Toronto: University of Toronto Press.

Paris, J (2006): *Half in Love with Death: Managing the Chronically Suicidal Patient.* New Jersey: Laurence Erlbaum.

Paris, J (2008a): *Prescriptions for the Mind: A Critical View of Contemporary Psychiatry.* New York: Oxford University Press.

Paris, J (2008b): *Treatment of Borderline Personality Disorder: A Guide to Evidence-Based Practice.* New York: Guilford Press.

Paris, J, Zweig-Frank, H (2001): A 27-year follow-up of patients with borderline personality disorder. *Comprehensive Psychiatry* 42: 482–487.

Parker, G, Fletcher, K (2007): Treating depression with the evidence-based psychotherapies: a critique of the evidence. *Acta Psychiatrica Scandinavica* 115: 352–359.

Pendergrast, M (1996): *Victims of Memory*, Second edition. Hinesburg, Vermont Upper Access.
Perls, F (1969): *Ego, Hunger, and Aggression: The Beginning of Gestalt Therapy*. New York: Random House.
Person, E (2007): *Dreams of Love and Fateful Encounters: The Power of Romantic Passion*. Washington DC: American Psychiatric Press.
Pinker, S (2002): *The Blank Slate: The Modern Denial of Human Nature*. New York: Viking.
Pinker, S (2011): *The Better Angels of Our Nature: Why Violence Has Declined*. New York: Viking.
Piper, WE, Rosie, JS, Joyce, AS (1996): *Time-Limited Day Treatment for Personality Disorders: Integration of Research and Practice in a Group Program*. Washington DC: American Psychological Association.
Pollak, M (1998): *The Creation of Dr. B: A Biography of Bruno Bettelheim*. New York: Simon and Schuster.
Pope, HJ, Jr. (1997): *Psychology Astray: Fallacies in Studies of "Repressed Memory" and Childhood Trauma*. Boca Raton, FL: Upton.
Putnam, RD (2000): *Bowling Alone: The Collapse and Revival of American Community*. New York: Simon & Schuster.
Person, E (2007): *Dreams of Love And Fateful Encounters: The Power of Romantic Passion*, 2nd edition, Washington DC: American Psychiatric Press.
Plomin, R, DeFries, JC, McClearn, GE, Rutter, M (2001): *Behavioral Genetics*, 4th edition. New York: Freeman.
Prager, K (1997): *The Psychology of Intimacy*. New York, Guilford.
Pressman, S (1993): *Outrageous Betrayal: The Real Story of Werner Erhard from Est to Exile*. New York: St. Martin's Press.
Prince, R, Tseng-Laroche, F (1990): Culture-bound syndromes and international disease classification. *Culture, Medicine, and Psychiatry* 11: 1–49.
Prochaska, JO, Norcross, JC, DiClemente, CC (1994): *Changing for Good*. New York: William Morrow.
Propst, A, Paris, J, Rosberger, Z (1994): Do therapist experience, diagnosis, and functional level predict outcome in short-term psychotherapy? *Canadian Journal of Psychiatry* 39: 178–183.
Rand, A (1961): *For the New Intellectual*. New York: Random House.
Raskin, R, Terry, H (1988): A principle-components analysis of the narcissistic personality inventory and further evidence of its construct validity. *Journal of Personality and Social Psychology* 54: 890–902.
Raup, JL, Myers, JE (1989): Empty nest syndrome: myth or reality? *Journal of Counseling & Development* 68: 180–183.
Reder, P, McClure, M, Jolley, A, (Eds.) (2000): *Family Matters: Interfaces Between Child and Adult Mental Health*. London: Routledge.
Remafedi, G (1999): Sexual orientation and youth suicide. *JAMA* 282: 1291–1292.
Rieber, R (2006): *The Bifurcation of the Self*. New York: Springer.
Rieff, P (1966): *The Triumph of the Therapeutic: Uses of Faith After Freud*. New York: Harper and Row.
Riesman, D, Glazer, N, Denney, R (2000): *The Lonely Crowd, Revised Edition: A Study of the Changing American Character*. New Haven: Yale University Press.
Roberts, BW, Helson, R (1997): Changes in culture, changes in personality the influence of individualism in a longitudinal study of women. *Journal of Personality and Social Psychology* 72: 641–651.

Robins, LN, Regier, DA (Eds) (1991): *Psychiatric Disorders in America.* New York: Free Press.

Rogers, C (1951): *Client-Centered Therapy: Its Current Practice, Implications and Theory.* London, UK: Constable.

Ronningstam, E (Ed.) (1998): *Disorders of Narcissism: Diagnostic, Clinical, and Empirical Implications.* Washington DC: American Psychiatric Press.

Ronningstam, E (2005): *Identifying and Understanding the Narcissistic Personality.* New York: Oxford University Press.

Rosen, RD (1977): *Psychobabble: Fast Talk and Quick Cure in the Era of Feeling.* New York: Atheneum.

Rosenberg, M (1965): *Society and the Adolescent Self-Image.* Princeton, NJ: Princeton University Press.

Roth, A, Fonagy, P (2005): *What Works For Whom?: A Critical Review of Psychotherapy Research,* 2nd edition. New York: Guilford.

Russ, E, Shedler, J, Bradley, R, Westen, D (2008): Refining the construct of narcissistic personality disorder: diagnostic criteria and subtypes. *American Journal of Psychiatry* 165: 1473–1481.

Rutter, M (2007): *Genes and Behavior: Nature-Nurture Interplay Explained.* London: Blackwell.

Rutter, M, Rutter, M (1993): *Developing Minds: Challenge and Continuity Across the Life Span.* New York: Basic.

Rutter, M, Smith, DJ (1995): *Psychosocial Problems in Young People.* Cambridge: UK: Cambridge University Press.

Ryder, AG, Yang, J, Zhu, X, Yao, S, Yi, J, Heine, SJ, Bagby, RM (2008): The cultural shaping of depression: somatic symptoms in China, psychological symptoms in North America? *Journal of Abnormal Psychology* 11: 300–313.

Sackett, DL, Richardson, WS, Rosenberg, W, Haynes, RB (1997): *Evidence-Based Medicine.* Edinburgh: Churchill Livingstone.

Sahlins, M (1968): Notes on the original affluent society, In RB Lee, I DeVore (Eds), *Man the Hunter.* New York: Aldine, pp. 85–89.

Sandell, R, Blomberg, J, Lazar, A, Carlsson, J, Broberg, J, Schubert, J (2000): Varieties of long-term outcome among patients in psychoanalysis and long-term psychotherapy. *International Journal of Psychoanalysis* 81: 921–942.

Satel, S, Sommers, CH (2005): *One Nation Under Therapy: How the Helping Culture is Eroding Self-Reliance.* New York: St. Martin's Press.

Sato, T, Takeichi, M (1993): Lifetime prevalence of specific psychiatric disorders in a general medicine clinic. *General Hospital Psychiatry* 15: 224–233.

Schamma, S (2008): *The American Future.* New York: Penguin.

Schacter, DL (1996): *Searching for Memory.* New York: Basic.

Schofield, P (1964): *Psychotherapy: The Purchase of Friendship.* New York: Prentice Hall.

Schoen, R, Astone, NM, Rothert, K, Standish, NJ, Young, JK (2002): Women's employment, marital happiness, and divorce. *Social Forces* 81: 643–650.

Schreiber, FR (1973): *Sybil.* Chicago, IL: Regnery.

Schuster, DG (2003): Neurasthenia and a modernizing America. *JAMA* 17: 2327–2328.

Segal, ZV, Williams, MG, Teasdale, JD (2002): *Mindfulness-Based Cognitive Therapy for Depression: A New Approach to Preventing Relapse.* New York: Guilford Press.

Seidler, GH, Wagner, FE (2006): Comparing the efficacy of EMDR and trauma-focused cognitive-behavioral therapy in the treatment of PTSD: A meta-analytic study. *Psychological Medicine* 36: 1515–1522.
Seligman, MEP (1995): The effectiveness of psychotherapy: the consumer reports study. *American Psychologist* 50: 965–974.
Shapiro, F (1995): *Eye Movement Desensitization and Reprocessing: Basic Principles, Protocols, and Procedures*. New York: Guilford Press.
Sharaf, M (1983): *Fury on Earth*. New York: St Martin's Press/Marek.
Shorter, E (1977): *The Making of the Modern Family*. New York: Basic.
Shorter, E (1994): *From the Mind into the Body: Cultural Origins of Psychosomatic Disorders*. New York: Free Press.
Shorter, E (1997): *A History of Psychiatry*. New York: John Wiley.
Showalter, E (1997): *Hystories: Hysterical Epidemics and Modern Culture*. New York: Columbia University Press.
Sijbrandji, B, Olff, M, Reitsma, JB, Carlier, IVE, Gerson, BPR (2006): Emotional or educational debriefing after psychological trauma: randomized controlled trial. *British Journal of Psychiatry* 189: 150–155.
Slovenko, R (1998): *Psychotherapy and Confidentiality: Testimonial Privileged Communication, Breach of Confidentiality, and Reporting Duties*. New York: Charles C. Thomas.
Smith, ML, Glass, GV, Miller, T (1980): *The Benefits of Psychotherapy*. Baltimore: Johns Hopkins Press.
Sokal, A, Bricmont, J (2007): *Fashionable Nonsense: Postmodern Intellectuals' Abuse of Science*. London: St. Martin's Press.
Sommers, CH, Satel, S (2005): *One Nation Under Therapy: How the Helping Culture is Eroding Self-Reliance*. New York: St. Martin's Press.
Southall, A (1998): *The City in Time and Space*. Cambridge, UK: Cambridge University Press.
Spock, B (1998): *Baby and Child Care*. New York: Pocket Books.
Stendahl, H (1822/1983): *On Love*. New York: Da Capo Press.
Sternberg, RJ (1988): *The Triangle of Love: Intimacy, Passion, Commitment*. New York: Basic Books.
Stinson, FS, Dawson, DA, Goldstein, RB, Chou, SP, Huang, B, Smith, SM, Ruan, WJ, Pulay, AJ, Saha, TD, Pickering, RP, Grant, BF (2008): Prevalence, correlates, disability, and comorbidity of DSM-IV narcissistic personality disorder: results from the wave 2 national epidemiologic survey on alcohol and related conditions. *Journal of Clinical Psychiatry* 69: 1033–1045.
Stone, MH (2006): *Personality-Disordered Patients: Treatable and Untreatable*. Washington DC: American Psychiatric Press.
Strean, HS (1974): *The Social Worker as Psychotherapist*. Metuchin, N.J.: Scarecrow Press.
Strow, CW, Strow, BK (2006): A history of divorce and remarriage in the United States. *Humanomics* 22: 239–257.
Strupp, HH, Fox, RE, Lesser, K (1969): *Patients View Their Psychotherapy*. Baltimore: Johns Hopkins.
Strupp, HH, Hadley, SW, Gomez-Schwartz, B (1977): *Psychotherapy for Better or Worse: The Problem of Negative Effects*. New York: Jason Aronson.
Strupp, HH, Hadley, SW (1979): Specific vs. non-specific factors in psychotherapy. *Archives of General Psychiatry* 36: 1125–1136.

Sundberg, N (2001). *Clinical Psychology: Evolving Theory, Practice, and Research.* Englewood Cliffs: Prentice Hall.

Sykes, CJ (1992): *A Nation Of Victims: The Decay of the American Character.* New York: St. Martin's Press.

Symons, D (1979): *The Evolution of Human Sexuality* New York, Oxford University Press.

Tannen, D (1990): *You Just Don't Understand: Women and Men in Conversation.* New York: William Morrow.

Tarrier, N (2005): Cognitive behaviour therapy for schizophrenia—a review of development, evidence and implementation. *Psychotherapy & Psychosomatics* 74: 136–144.

Taylor, C (1989): *Sources of the Self: The Making of the Modern Identity.* Cambridge, MA: Harvard University Press.

Taylor, C (1991): *The Malaise of Modernity*, Toronto: Anansi.

Taylor, C (2007): *A Secular Age.* Cambridge, MA: Harvard University Press.

Tennow, D (1999): *Love and Limerence: The Experience of Being in Love.* New York: Scarborough House.

The National Marriage Project (2000): *The State of Our Unions 2000: The Social Health of Marriage in America.* New Brunswick, NJ: The National Marriage Project.

Thomaes, S, Bushman, BJ, Orobio De Castro, B, Stegge, H (2009): What makes narcissists bloom? A framework for research on the etiology and development of narcissism. *Development and Psychopathology* 21: 1233–1247.

Tocqueville, A (1835/2000): *Democracy in America*, H Mansfield, D Winthrop (Trans.). Chicago: University of Chicago Press.

Tolkien, JRR (1991): *The Lord of the Rings.* New York: HarperCollins.

Tonnies, F (2001): *Community and Civil Society*, Jose Harris, Jose Harris, Margaret Hollis (Trans.). Cambridge, UK: Cambridge University Press.

Tooby, J, Cosmides, L (1990): On the universality of human nature and the uniqueness of the individual: The role of genetics and adaptation. *Journal of Personality* 58: 17–67.

Torrey, EF (1992): *Freudian Fraud: The Malignant Effect of Freud's Theory on American Thought and Culture.* New York: Harper Collins.

Trzesniewski, KH, Donnellan, MB, Robins, RW (2008): Do today's young people really think they are so extraordinary? An examination of secular trends in narcissism and self-enhancement. *Psychological Science* 19: 181–188.

Tsai, JL, Butcher, JN, Munoz, RF, Vitousek, K (2001): Culture, ethnicity, and psychopathology. In HC Adams, PB Sutker (Eds), *Comprehensive Handbook of Psychopathology* pp. 105–127. New York: Kluwer Academic/Plenum.

Tseng, W-S (1999): Culture and psychotherapy: review and practical guidelines. *Transcultural Psychiatry* 36: 131–179.

Turkington, D, Kingdon, D, Weiden, PJ (2006): Cognitive behavior therapy for schizophrenia. *American Journal of Psychiatry* 163: 365–373.

Turner, BS (2004): Religion, romantic love, and the family, In JL Scott, J Treas, M Richards (Eds), *The Blackwell Companion to the Sociology of Families.* London: Blackwell, pp. 289–305.

Twenge, JM (2006): *Generation Me: Why Today's Young Americans Are More Confident, Assertive, Entitled—and More Miserable Than Ever Before.* New York: Free Press.

Twenge, JM (2011): Culture and narcissism, In WK Campbell, J Miller (Eds), *Handbook of Narcissism and Narcissistic Personality Disorder*. New York: Wiley, pp. 202–209.

Twenge, JM, Foster, JD (2008): Mapping the scale of the narcissism epidemic: increases in narcissism 2002–2007 within ethnic groups. *Journal of Research in Personality* 42: 1619–1622.

Twenge, JM, Campbell, WK (2009): *The Narcissism Epidemic: Living in the Age of Entitlement.* New York: Simon and Schuster.

Twenge, JM, Foster, JD (2010): Birth cohort increases in narcissistic personality traits among American college students, 1982–2009. *Social Psychological and Personality Science* 1: 99–106.

U'Ren, R (2011): *Social Perspective.* Toronto: University of Toronto Press.

Vaillant, GE (1977): *Adaptation to Life.* Cambridge MA: Little Brown.

Vaillant, GE (2002): *Aging Well: Surprising Guideposts to a Happier Life from the Landmark Harvard Study of Adult Development.* New York: Little Brown.

Waite, LJ, Gallagher, M (2000): *The Case for Marriage: Why Married People are Happier.* New York: Doubleday.

Wallerstein, J (1989): *Second Chances: Men, Women, and Children a Decade after Divorce.* New York: Ticknor and Fields.

Wallerstein, R (1986): *Forty-two Lives in Treatment.* New York: Guilford.

Walmsley, DJ (1988): *Urban Living: The Individual in the City.* Harlow UK: Longman Scientific & Technical.

Wampold, BE (2001): *The Great Psychotherapy Debate: Models, Methods, and Findings.* Mahwah, N.J.: Erlbaum Associates.

Wampold, BE (2007): Psychotherapy: *The* humanistic (and effective) treatment. *American Psychologist* 62: 857–873.

Weber, M (1918): *Science as a Vocation,* http://www.ne.jp/asahi/moriyuki/abukuma/weber/lecture/science_frame.html, accessed June 2009.

Webster, S (1995): *Why Freud Was Wrong.* New York: Basic.

Wedding, D (2007): An international perspective on psychotherapy. *Journal of Clinical Psychology* 63: 785–790.

Weissman, MM, Klerman, GL (1993). *New Applications of Interpersonal Therapy.* Washington, DC: American Psychiatric Press.

Weissman, MM, Verdeli, H, Gameroff, MJ, Bledsoe, SE, Betts, K, Mufson, L (2006): National survey of psychotherapy training in psychiatry, psychology, and social work. *Archives of General Psychiatry* 63: 925–934.

Westen, D (1988): *Self and Society: Narcissism, Collectivism, and the Development of Morals.* New York: Cambridge University Press.

Westen, D (1998): The scientific legacy of Sigmund Freud: towards a psychodynamically informed psychological science. *Psychological Bulletin* 124: 128–136.

White, LK (1990): Determinants of divorce: a review of research in the eighties. *Journal of Marriage and the Family* 52: 904–912.

Whitehead, BD (1997): *The Divorce Culture: Rethinking Our Commitments to Marriage and Family.* New York: Knopf.

Wilkinson, RW, Pickett, K (2009): *The Spirit Level: Why More Equal Societies Almost Always Do Better.* London: Allen Lane.

Wilson. E (2003): *Bohemians: The Glamorous Outcasts.* New York: Tauris Parke.

Wilson, JQ (2002): *The Marriage Problem: How Our Culture Has Weakened Families.* New York: HarperCollins.
Wink, P, Dillon, M, Fay, K (2005): Spiritual seeking, narcissism, and psychotherapy: how are they related? *Journal for the Scientific Study of Religion* 44: 143–158.
Wolfe, T (1975): *The Painted Word.* New York: Farrar, Straus and Giroux.
Wolfe, T (1976): The me decade and the third great awakening. *New York Magazine*, August 23.
Wolpe, J (1973): *The Practice of Behavior Therapy,* 2nd edition. New York: Pergamon Press.
Wood, ND, Crane, DR, Schaakjem GB, Law, DD (2005): What works for whom: a meta-analytic review of marital and couples therapy in reference to marital distress, *American Journal of Family Therapy* 33: 273–287.
Wortis, J (1984): *Fragments of an Analysis with Freud.* New York: Jason Aronson.
Wright, R (2000): *The Moral Animal: Why We Are, the Way We Are: The New Science of Evolutionary Psychology*, New York: Random House.
Wright, R (2008): *What is America?* New York: Penguin.
Yalom, I, Lescz, M (2005): *The Theory and Practice of Psychotherapy.* New York: Basic Books.
Young, A (1995): *The Harmony of Illusions: Inventing Posttraumatic Stress Disorder.* Princeton, NJ: Princeton University Press.
Zaretsky, E (2004): *Secrets of the Soul: A Social and Cultural History of Psychoanalysis.* New York: Knopf.
Zerbetto, R, Tantam, D (2001): The survey of European psychotherapy training 3: what psychotherapy is available in Europe? *European Journal of Psychotherapy & Counselling* 4: 397–405.
Zimmerman, M, Chelminski, I, Young, D (2008): The frequency of personality disorders in psychiatric patients. *Psychiatric Clinics of North America* 31: 405–420.
Zimring, FE (2006): *The Great American Crime Decline.* New York: Oxford University Press.

Index

Printed and bound in the United States of America